The Handoff

To "Kenny for the moon"

Thanks for listening!

Thanks for your support!

J.T. The Brick

The Handoff

A Memoir of Two Guys,
Sports, and Friendship

JOHN "JT THE BRICK"
TOURNOUR
AND ALAN EISENSTOCK

CENTER
STREET

New York Boston Nashville

Center Street
Hachette Book Group
237 Park Avenue
New York, NY 10017

www.CenterStreet.com

Printed in the United States of America

RRD-C

First edition: August 2013
10 9 8 7 6 5 4 3 2 1

Center Street is a division of Hachette Book Group, Inc.
The Center Street name and logo are trademarks of Hachette Book Group, Inc.

The Hachette Speakers Bureau provides a wide range of authors for speaking events. To find out more, go to www.HachetteSpeakersBureau.com or call (866) 376-6591.

The publisher is not responsible for websites (or their content) that are not owned by the publisher.

ISBN 978-1-4555-2790-8

Library of Congress Control Number: 2013934143

This book is dedicated with love and gratitude to Mom,
Dad, Julie, John, and Jason—and Andrew

Contents

Author's Note

This work is a memoir. Some names and identifying details of certain people have been changed and a few individuals are composites. In some instances, the precise details or timing of events have been changed to assist with the flow of the narrative.

The Handoff

1.

Walking the Empty Halls of Hope

Saturday, September 1, 2012
11:13 a.m.
Nearly Four Years Later

IN THE RENTED SUV I drive the four-lane freeway to the city of Duarte, hugging the right lane, taking my time, taking it all in again, the endless fast-food franchises, the boxy rain-stained office buildings, the sprawling car dealerships, the sinister collision centers with funnels of steam rising from their chain-link-enclosed blacktops. I pull off at an exit and turn onto a narrow street lined with stucco shacks packed in tight, a satellite dish on every roof making me feel as if I've infiltrated some kind of metallic, alien Cyclops colony.

I stop at a red light. As I wait for the light to change, my stomach clenches. It hits me now through a stab of memory, a jagged ripping of my heart. This drive. All those drives. The jittery nerves that dug into me that first time as Andrew, swallowing his own fear, I'm sure, covered it up by railing about something or other coming through the radio, a voice we knew, gravelly, loud, spewing an outlandish sports opinion, or melodic, soothing, crooning the play-by-play of some game.

He's calming me down, I thought that first time. *Putting me at ease. Supposed to be the other way around. He's the one with cancer.*

"It'll be all right," he said, reading my mood like a teleprompter.

"Oh, yeah," I said, drumming the steering wheel with a finger, my eyes looking off, avoiding his, my stomach tightening.

"It will be. We're gonna beat this thing, JT. Gonna kick its *ass*."

He meant it. With all his heart. He imagined these drives to chemotherapy as pregame warm-ups or battle prep. We were linemen banging each other's shoulder pads before kickoff or, more aptly, boxers ducking into the ring for a championship bout. We were warriors preparing to charge, fight, kill, maim, disembowel, *eviscerate* this motherfucking cancer.

"Winning is my only option," he said continually, his mantra, repeated to everyone who knew about his diagnosis.

And yet on many drives, especially toward the end, primed for my role as Robin to his Batman, hit man to his mob boss, general to his commander in chief, I would sense Andrew's energy sag. I would feel less a warrior than a driver, a chauffeur, his wingman at the wheel who had his back but had no power, none at all. I wanted to be a superhero. I wanted to save him, or at least be his enforcer. I would've done anything to carry out the hit on his motherfucking cancer. But the gun sounded ending the fourth quarter, the bell rang stopping the bout, the battle ran out of steam, and the warriors retreated, and all I could do was watch and comfort him. And drive him.

Ultimately, I did do more. I learned from him. When the battleground shifted and the tide turned and we both knew without saying anything that he'd lost, he changed the focus. If this were a football game, he reversed strategy from the long bomb, a Hail Mary, to a handoff. Andrew had much to hand off to me in too short a time, a lifetime's worth of wisdom—a lifetime of *living*—in little more than a year. In order to take it all in, to absorb all he held in his heart, these lessons he was determined to pass on to me, I had to change, to make myself over, and quickly. I had to perform a one-eighty, a complete turnaround, a total revolution. I was working well above my pay grade. I felt as if I had to undo my DNA. I had to transform myself from a self-absorbed nonstop talker to a quiet and keen listener, from a Hall of Fame narcissist to a world-class giver, from a wall-crashing lunatic to a calm and cool observer. We both knew I was a work in progress—well, we all are—but having once been Andrew's project on the radio, raw but willing, I had now become his project in life as well as his primary chemotherapy partner and designated spokesperson to his close community of friends and coworkers. He chose me because he knew he could count on me. He knew I would show up every day, upbeat and positive, and that I could read his moods, get him to laugh when he appeared ready to slide too far downhill, inform him of anything he needed to know in the radio world he ruled, where I, too, worked. And he knew I would shut up when he required quiet to reflect, to remember, or just to be.

In other words, I knew him, and cherished him, and Andrew knew that and relied on that. He trusted me with his life. And his death.

He knew I was eager to learn, not by asking questions but simply by observing. He saw in me reflections of himself, not the least of which thrummed a consuming need to *connect*, at all times, professionally and personally, to listeners on the air and loved ones in our lives. We both got ultimate fulfillment by matching people up and putting them together and then watching them click. Andrew did it for me constantly, joyfully, connecting me to Tomm Looney, my cohost of nine years on the radio, to the Oakland Raiders, today going on sixteen years, and to the woman who saved me, my wife of fourteen years, on that magical and fateful night in which we sat ringside literally at the feet of the Rolling Stones, doused liberally by showers of Mick Jagger's spit. I called Andrew the King Kong of Connectors. He wore the title like a championship belt. At the end, wordlessly and happily, he passed on that honor to me, confident I was worthy to carry on connecting in his name, the first of many handoffs.

"We don't have much time," he said on one drive when we were running late, his voice cracking. I thought he was referring to his appointment, but when I caught the sparkle in his eyes, which he slowly closed before tilting his head back against the seat, I knew he meant something else, something more.

This September morning the red light changes and I turn left and watch the small stucco houses disappear on the right side to be replaced by a wide swath of green, a park, a lush botanical garden, or well-tended college campus. In a few seconds, I turn right into the middle of this green, the entrance to City of Hope, world-famous cancer facility. Flowers bloom everywhere, full-branched trees provide shade and cover. The setting for this renowned medical center is not stark or sterile and only hints at a hospital being there. The grounds feel inviting and comfortable and safe.

As I drive toward the main building, I pull into the familiar turnaround past a cluster of wheelchairs crushed together in what looks like a cross between a bicycle rack and bumper car holding pen. On good days I would stop at the curb, and Andrew, the man once nicknamed Gorilla, would maneuver his 300-pound frame out of the SUV and take a seat on a park bench. He'd wave while I pulled away and found a spot in the nearby parking lot. I'd catch him in the rearview mirror, his head rising to catch the sun, his resemblance to the late John Candy striking. On other days, the not-so-good days, I would stop at the curb, hop out of the SUV, run over to his side, help him out, settle him into a wheelchair, and lock it down. I'd ease over to the parking lot, checking him all the way in the rearview mirror. On those days, he would stare blankly forward or lower his head and gaze onto the pavement, shoulders slumped, and he wouldn't wave.

This day, this Saturday four years after, the parking lot is eerily empty. I choose a space in the first row, near the wishing tree, a young, newly planted sapling. Dozens of strips of construction paper, all different colors, hang off the tree's thin branches like leaves. Each strip contains a wish for a patient in City of Hope and was written by a loved one, or sometimes by a staff member. I don't remember the wishing tree. I don't think it existed four years ago. If it had, Andrew's loved ones would have filled a forest of wishing trees.

I step down from the SUV and head into the main reception area. A woman in uniform sits at a horseshoe counter behind a desk. I walk toward her and a lump lodges in my throat.

"Hello," she says, all smiles, as if she's working check-in at the front desk of a hotel. "Can I help you?"

"I used to know somebody who—"

That's all I manage to get out. It's all she needs.

"Of course," she says, her voice lower, the smile lost. "You can walk around. Kind of quiet today."

I clear my throat, dislodging the lump. "Thank you."

I want to tell her that I'm on a mission, a mission to remember, but I don't have to. I meet her eyes and she understands.

I walk through reception, down a corridor to an open area and a wall of elevators. I take an elevator to the third floor, come out to a lobby with a white tile floor leading into a smaller reception area, a waiting room I remember vividly, now empty, dark, cold, and smelling faintly of disinfectant. I stop at the entrance to the room and scan the line of chairs that border the walls. I walk over to a counter at the far right side and see a name plaque with HEATHER in cursive lettering, and in my mind I hear Andrew's voice.

"Yeah, babe!"

Suddenly I see the room filled with patients, caregivers, chemo partners, stricken kids and suffering parents, elderly wives and husbands, people with hollowed, frightened faces and sunken eyes. Above a low-level hum of voices straining to find some hope or relief or answers, Andrew's voice comes at me again, a voice that crashes through the doom I feel in the empty room, smashing it to dust.

"How you doing, Heather, how are you?"

"Good, Andrew, good. How are you?"

"I'm so good. Hey, I'm *here*, right? Ha! Hanging in, hanging *in*. Yeah, babe!"

I would hang back, press into the wall, and watch Andrew operate, the life force rumbling through his hefty shoulders, a fresh fuse of energy ignited no matter how shitty he felt, stepping up to the plate, somehow able to turn off his pain and turn on his charm, and they would talk, Heather and Andrew, receptionist and cancer patient, as if they were at a bar or a party, and soon, without fail, they would laugh—Heather giggling, Andrew roaring—and in those few astonishing moments, the waiting room would be crackling with *life*.

Andrew's voice fades into silence. I turn and walk out, leaving the dark and emptiness and chill behind.

I prowl the corridor leading to a room marked PHARMACY, a stop we routinely made for meds. I picture us waiting in line, moving agonizingly slowly, inching, shuffling forward, Andrew sometimes standing with me, sometimes giving up and landing in a chair off to the side, his expression dazed, frozen, looking ahead at nothing.

I return to the elevator, step inside, and punch a button. The elevator goes down a level and the doors open. I take one step out and stop, confused. This level is under construction, drop cloths on the floor, walls tagged over with heavy paper marked with blue pencil. It takes a moment, but then I realize where I am, where I wanted to be. Infusion. I walk down a hallway, veer right past a wall of examination rooms, then arrive at the infusion center, which today is locked. I shade my eyes and peer through the small square window in the door. My view is blocked, but my memory is clear. Here it happened—infusion—where Andrew took the chemo, bags of clear watery liquid disguising the potent poison pumped into his arm and aimed to shrink and possibly, hopefully, wipe out the cancer cells. A squadron of tiny liquid drones. The procedure took hours. We'd arrive with our laptops. He'd set up in the hospital bed, boot up, and jump in, e-mailing, working, consulting, *connecting* as he took the chemo. I'd arrange myself across a couple of chairs. Some days Andrew would work intently, turning his chemo room into his office, an away game. We'd spend much of the time in silence, lost in the glow of our respective blue screens. Occasionally he'd doze, and I'd move his laptop next to me to prevent it from tumbling off the bed.

Inevitably a time would come during each session, at least once, often more, that all this would overwhelm me. An hour or two in, I would feel some inner part of me tremble—in discomfort, fear, exhaustion, or disbelief—and I would need to get away.

"Hey, man, I'm gonna get a coffee. You want anything?"

"No, thanks, I'm good." His voice would rise to meet mine, but I knew he felt his own, deeper discomfort, fear, exhaustion, or disbelief.

"Be right back."

I would push through the door of his hospital room and speed walk out of the infusion center, fighting an urge to plow through the next set of doors and sprint somewhere, anywhere, so I might catch my breath, regroup, realign my tangle of thoughts and feelings, and blow out my rage, yes, my fucking *rage* that this could be—was—actually happening, that this was real.

I'd end up at the snack bar, a small counter behind which a hospital employee sold snacks one tick above vending machine quality and thin black liquid passing as coffee. Half-assed nourishment for people like me, chemo partners on the run, desperate for a blow. I don't remember what, if anything, I ate, maybe a bagel, muffin, candy bar. I do remember firing up my cell phone and checking in with my own support system: Julie, Jimmy B., Bobby G., Looney, my producer Mike Pearson, my dad, and others on Andrew watch, Sandra, Jeff, Dresch. He had a long list of those waiting by the phone, wanting to hear a snippet of something resembling good news.

I would spend too much time away from him, I know. I didn't mean to. I meant to get right back in, to roll right back into the foxhole, to hustle back into the game. I just couldn't. I needed a break from the intensity. That's what I told myself. It was okay to sip a coffee, to pick at a rubbery blueberry muffin, to make calls. I deserved a break, didn't I?

No, actually, I didn't.

Andrew never got a break, never took a breather. You don't get a break from cancer. Cancer doesn't give you any time off.

Walking back through City of Hope that Saturday, stung by the silence, the lack of activity, the eerie hallways, vacant and noiseless except for my footsteps echoing off the walls, the emptiness of these corridors casting some kind of pall, feeling brutally alone and missing Andrew, missing him terribly, I think of a lesson I learned. It's not the obvious one, that cancer doesn't give you a break. The lessons Andrew taught me were always surprising. In this case, the lesson is that you can't give 100 percent all the time. That's impossible. Expecting perfection often leads to defeat. The lesson is *Do what you can.* It's okay if you can't do more. Just don't do less.

I climb behind the wheel of my rented SUV and stare at City of Hope, today a ghost city, and I take in the lush green grounds that front the buildings, twin care centers, and I think what a perfectly descriptive name this place has. This is truly a city of hope, and a city of wishes and memory and loss and love. Yes, cancer never takes time off, but cancer doctors and caregivers do. They must.

—

Andrew Ashwood—my boss, my mentor, my role model, my conscience, my dear friend, my *brother*—passed away on November 13, 2008.

He was fifty-one years old.

His obituary flooded the media and the Internet. Condolences packed my in-box and filled up my voice mail. *Fox NFL Sunday,* the number-one-rated pregame show, hosted by Curt Menefee with Terry Bradshaw, Howie Long, Michael Strahan, and Jimmy Johnson, led off that week's broadcast with a tribute to Andrew. Menefee opened by saying he had sad news to report and then told of Andrew's passing. He called Andrew a "valued colleague and mentor" and added: "He was truly—and I mean *truly*—a wonderful guy. Andrew Ashwood will sorely be missed."

A week or so later, Andrew's wife, Sandra, and a few of us put together a memorial service at Forest Lawn cemetery. Many people spoke. I spoke toward the end. I felt nervous and inadequate. I knew that nothing I said would do Andrew justice. I did the best I could. I read a section of Theodore Roosevelt's famous Courage speech and related it to Andrew's battle with cancer. I spoke of Andrew's inner strength, of how hard he fought, how he refused to give in to his disease, and how he believed that winning was his only option. I spoke with passion and with love and from my heart. The whole time I stood in front of the crowd at that memorial service I felt my pulse thumping. When I finished, I bolted back to my seat, fighting back tears. I didn't want to fall apart in front of everyone.

At the reception later, people came up to me and told me how much my words had moved them. Many thanked me for what I did for Andrew during the last months of his life. I shook my head and said that, in all honesty, I didn't do anything special for him. I was just being his friend.

Four years ago, when Andrew died, it didn't occur to me to write this story, the story of my life, the story of my life with Andrew and the lessons he taught me. I never took notes, wrote in a journal, or spoke into a tape recorder. I kept all these stories, all those feelings, inside. But now, slowly, I begin to process everything and starting with my story, humbly, I remember...

I let it all out and allow it to breathe.

2.

John, Who Becomes JT

Massapequa and Geneseo
1981–1987

I START WITH a question.

Who am I?

Well, if you listen to sports talk radio, you know me as JT the Brick.

I've been called the most energetic, most interactive, and loudest sports talk radio host in America.

Not true.

I'm only like the third loudest.

Here's how I often begin my show:

"OUT OF THE GATE…IT'S JT THE BRICK! SOUND OFF LIKE YOU GOT A PAIR!"

Outstanding, right? Yeah. Mr. Subtle. You can hear me every night syndicated on Fox Sports Radio from one a.m. until five a.m. (ten p.m. to two a.m. on the West Coast). I'm on pretty much everywhere—Los

Angeles, Chicago, Dallas, Houston, Boston, San Francisco, San Antonio, Seattle, Miami, Washington, D.C., Detroit, Cleveland, Atlanta, Nashville—more than two hundred stations across the country, as well as Sirius XM and the American Forces Network.

I'm sure you've heard me on the West Coast, especially if you're a football fan. I've been working for the Oakland Raiders for the past fifteen years, doing pregame, postgame, and now the weekly Raiders Report.

So, yes, I—JT the Brick—am going strong.

The thing is, though, JT the Brick is a character.

My alter ego.

A part I play.

Usually when it's the dead of night and I'm alone.

I became the Brick more than twenty years ago when I landed in San Diego.

I became JT in college at Geneseo, around the time that the DKs, my fraternity, the rowdiest, wildest band of brothers ever to host a kegger and trash a house, voted me president, an honor I cherish to this day.

But before that, growing up with my family in Massapequa, New York, I was just John.

———

Seven hours.

That's how long it will take, my dad predicts, to make the drive from Massapequa, Long Island, where I have lived my whole life, to Geneseo in upstate New York, just south of Rochester, where I will spend the next four years.

My dad drives, my mom rides shotgun. I sit in the backseat

feeling dazed, uprooted, and slightly hungover from last night's send-off party. I yawn and turn my neck toward the thruway behind me. I locate the pickup a couple of car lengths behind and I take a breath. Jimmy Baxter, my best friend, rides with Greg Eddy, another close friend, owner and driver of the pickup, a vehicle that served for much of our past two years as a kind of mobile party van. Now, in seven hours, we three will enter our freshman year at Geneseo State, the pickup our one tangible reminder of our former lives.

I turn back and contemplate the backs of my parents' heads, locked in position, unmoving, stoically focused at the road in front of them. I look out my window and try to take in the scenery, the rolling hills, fields as green as fairways, livestock nibbling on clumps of grass. Suddenly scenes from my life rush into my mind. I picture myself growing up in Massapequa and I realize that for so long, in particular through my high school years, I've led two lives.

During the week, I am John, the dutiful son, respectful follower of my dad's house rules, and popular high school swim star, elected captain of the team. I have been a competitive swimmer for seven or eight years—I've lost count—a youth spent underwater. Every day, Monday through Friday, and sometimes Saturdays, I undergo two or more grueling hours at swim practice or at swim meets. At some point—I'm not sure exactly when it happens—I lose my love for the sport, if I ever had it at all. I am done. I don't quit, that's not who I am, but I slowly become desensitized. Robotic. I plunge joylessly into the high school pool, my body feeling cut by the cold water as if by the steel blade of a knife. For the next several hours I stay submerged, restricted to my lane, my face down, my mouth closed. The only sound I hear is the rhythmic *whap-whap-whap* of my own body slicing through the water. I feel isolated, alone, and, increasingly, lost. I come home after swimming as late as seven or even eight o'clock if we have a meet, and while my wet clothes tumble and clank in the dryer I sit across from my sisters, Dana and Jill, competitive swimmers both, and pick at the dinner my mom has placed before me, my muscles throbbing with exhaustion. I study my plate and lose myself in silent questions that zip through my mind, most prominent among them *Who am I?* Followed by *What am I doing?* I excel at swimming, thrive on the competition, love to win, but I've come to despise the rest of it, the long hours, the endless mind-numbing practices, shaving my legs, my head, my armpits, but hate, most of all, the isolation. As I struggle to figure out my own identity and to see where I *fit*, I know this much. I am not a loner. I need people around me. I need the comfort and the strength I find in my friends, the brotherhood.

My best friend since forever and charter member of the brotherhood is Jimmy Baxter. We are as close as brothers, or at least as close as I imagine brothers can be. I envy my dad and his twin brother and how they mirror each other, the way they act, walk, talk, move, laugh, how they anticipate each other's thoughts, finish each other's sentences, how they *are*. I want that. I feel deprived of that. I want a brother who is that close.

Jimmy feels the same way. We cast each other in the role of each other's best friend early on, in elementary school, and become inseparable, to the point that Jimmy is a fixture at our Sunday family gatherings. He melds into the family, as close as my cousin Geno. Then right before we begin middle school, Jimmy announces that he is moving to another town and another school. I have heard of the place, but it has always seemed foreign and far away, in another world. He may as well be moving to Canada. I swallow the news like a dose of foul-tasting medicine, fearing that with this change we will lose our closeness, our brotherhood.

We don't let that happen. We beat the odds. We amp up our closeness, refuse to allow our friendship to fray. We sleep at each other's house every weekend. At first our parents drive us, then when we get older we ride our bikes, and then we drive a family car. Not only do we maintain our own brotherhood, we expand the membership, adding our separate circles of close friends. No alternative occurs to us. We are and always will be brothers.

The second life I lead, the one I conduct away from home under the cover of darkness—on some weeknights even before I turn sixteen and on every Friday and Saturday night—is the life of rebel party boy. Feeling constricted at home by my dad's rules and suffocated by my role as the good son, the good kid, and the tolerant brother, I bust out at night with my pack of friends. In the beginning, we hang with older kids, high school seniors, brothers of friends in my class. I sample beer and develop a taste for it while chasing mostly unavailable girls, many of them seniors, striking out mightily. We squeeze into any available spot in any car that offers us a ride, long sedans crammed with two or three kids over the limit. The cars jockey for position in circular drives fronting large houses overflowing with kids, rock music blaring, beer flowing, parents checked out or checked into hotels in the city or in the Bahamas or snowbirding in their condos in Florida. When these parties spread outside and out of control and the police arrive, we duck and run, Jimmy B. and the brotherhood following me, benefactors of my sixth sense of oncoming trouble. Eventually—perhaps after a kid's parents show up unannounced in the middle of some debauchery and shut everything down—we spill out of the suburban mansions and into the woods, where we build forts. Serious forts. Elaborate forts. A far cry from the little structures we made out of twigs and burlap bags when we were ten and playing Army.

We find a clearing in the woods, bring out shovels, and dig a massive hole, wide and deep enough to hold twenty or more people. We line the hole with wood framing to hold back the dirt. Then we build a roof and lay a tarp on top of that. We even fashion a door and secure it with a combination lock confiscated from somebody's locker. We furnish the inside of the fort with blankets, old mattresses, a boom box, and cases of beer purchased by some older kid at the local 7-Eleven. The night of the fort party, usually a Friday or Saturday, we huddle in the 7-Eleven parking lot waiting for an older kid to return with at least four cases, hoping that he doesn't shortchange us or take a cut off the top for his commission.

At the start of the party, Lynyrd Skynyrd, Led Zeppelin, or Rush cranking from the boom box, girls everywhere, hot, loose, and hopefully drunk, Jimmy and I, the leaders, build a fire in front of the fort. We gather armfuls of kindling and stray logs from the woods, pile them up, drizzle lighter fluid, and light a match. *Whoosh.* Within seconds, blue flames rage.

Looking back at this insanity, I feel ridiculously lucky that we never started a forest fire. We also somehow avoided getting busted by the police, who could have hauled us in on numerous charges—endangering a natural habitat, disturbing the peace, trespassing, drunk and disorderly, fooling around with minors, fooling around with *fire*, and for just being, in general, stupid.

"How you doing back there, John? You okay?"

In the backseat, I blink to get my bearings and snap back into the present. "Yeah, Dad, I'm good."

"They still with us?"

I duck my head to get a good look out the back window and locate the pickup, still maintaining its two-car-length distance. I glimpse Eddy's long hair bobbing as he drives, imagining him and Jimmy lost in the groove of some song blasting through the truck's radio as they tail us.

"Yep. Right behind us."

"Okay, good."

I yawn again. "Think I'm gonna take a nap."

My dad peers at me in the rearview mirror. "Good idea," he says.

I close my eyes but I can't sleep. I change position, lean my head against the car window, and, slowly, a kind of mental haze overtakes me, accompanied by slow, deep breaths. Suddenly, with the pavement rumbling beneath me, a dull whir causing me to fall into semiconsciousness, I review the CliffsNotes version of my life and allow that I've had it pretty good: a large, comfortable house in a safe neighborhood, a group of great friends, a couple of younger sisters whom I love to torment, a houseful of family, aunts, uncles, and cousins who arrive Sunday afternoons bearing platters of delicious food that we devour after a raucous round-robin of touch football or pickup base-ball games, my cousin Geno, my dad's twin brother's son, not an actual brother but as close as I'm going to get, and, yes, I also admit, parents who don't suck.

Eventually, through my late teens, twenties, and into my thirties, I will actually appreciate my parents perhaps more than most kids do, marveling at my mom, how she kept the family running like a fine-tuned machine, a woman who's a marvel of self-restraint and cool, doling out unlimited amounts of care, concern, and love; and revering my dad, my hero, role model, former high school superjock, now neighborhood legend, in-demand Little League coach, responsible wage earner, and a no bullshit but fair disciplinarian, distributor of what has become known as tough love. Even when I stray far from what may seem a TV sitcom upbringing or Norman Rockwell painting, falling into a period of my life that some may call a twenty-year frat party, I carry in my mind a picture of myself as the patri-arch of a family of my own, longing to measure up to my dad. Even as I trip and stumble and generally fuck up, during the rare moments that I consider my cloudy future, the words I see emblazoned next to my name, always, are *Family Man* and *Dad*.

And then, before I know it, before I can even grasp the pas-sage of time, my dad takes the Geneseo exit to Court Street and the campus, and I come to both the end and the beginning.

—

A swell of station wagons and rented vans stuffed with parents and teenagers sharing backseats with duffel bags. Neil Young squawking out of dorm room windows swallowed up by Aero-smith shaking dilapidated houses on fraternity row. Guys out-numbered by girls, four to one, many in tight T-shirts with GENESEO on the front.

Welcome to college.

As I step out of the car, my knees buckle in anticipation. My mom cranes her neck, her lips pursed, and my dad studies the campus quad, standing frozen for the moment as I pop the trunk. Jimmy exits the pickup, which Greg parks behind us, and Jimmy and I hoist out suitcases, duffels, his stereo, my TV, his guitar and amp.

"This is gonna be all right," I say, low.

"Best four years of your life," Jimmy says, eyeing a blonde coed strutting by in short shorts and a bikini top.

"Erie Hall," my dad says, consulting a signpost, steering us away from a line of girls sunbathing on the lawn. "Your dorm's this way."

"You were right," I say to my dad. "This is a good school."

"The Harvard of upstate New York," Jimmy says, discovering the sunbathers on the lawn and heading toward them, allegedly on the way to his dorm.

In my minuscule dorm room, I choose the bed on the left and my mom attacks the matzo-thin mattress with freshly laundered linens. My dad studies the room, his accountant's eyes analyzing its prison-cell size and decor, then wanders over to the far end of the bed to help my mom tuck in the mattress pad. I don't offer to help. I sense my parents' need to do this for me, especially my mom's. I see in her face a closemouthed look of determination and in her eyes something more, maybe a feeling of loss, or finality, or a last gasp of mothering before letting go. I feel all of this, but most of all, I feel that I am about to be released.

In the hall a girl squeals, a guy laughs, footsteps break into a run, and a chase begins, the kind of foreplay that in my experience always leads to an extremely good time.

"You are here to get an education," my dad reminds me, his forehead furrowed.

"Oh, definitely," I say, but my legs feel wobbly again. I long to get out into the hall and join the chase, or start one of my own. I reach for the sheet my mother tosses onto the bed. "Here, Mom, let me help."

"It's okay," she says, meaning *I want to do this, I have to do this.*

"Four years," my dad says, rocking back on his heels. "That's the deal. You have to graduate in four years."

"I know," I say. "I get that."

He nods. And like helpless, clueless bystanders, we watch my mom fold the sheets into hospital corners.

"Geneseo is highly rated," my dad adds randomly, as if validating his decision. Eight months ago, he sat across from Jimmy and me in his study and in a solemn voice listed our options for college, Geneseo being number one on a short wish list. He registered serious concern that I would be able to get in, my C+ average apparently a stumbling block.

"Captain of the swim team," my dad said. "I'm going to start there."

He made a call, wrote a letter, pulled some strings—I'll never know—and somehow Jimmy and I both got in.

"This is it!" Another dad's voice booms from outside the room, and then my roommate enters carrying an armful of stuff.

His stepdad—I'll learn later—follows with suitcases. He places them on the unmade bed and, without a glance at me or my parents, reaches into his pocket and pulls out a couple of bills, which he presses into my roommate's palm.

"So, hey, you're all set," the stepdad says. "Go have a good time."

A half grin to us and he's gone.

My roommate offers up a similar half smile to me and then extends his hand. "Hi," he says. "Michael Gerber."

I introduce myself and my parents and then Gerber and I begin decorating the dorm room's walls with posters. My mom finishes making the bed. Fighting back tears, she folds me into a hug, then breaks away to blow her nose. My dad rests one hand on my shoulder and with his other hand pumps mine as if I've won some kind of major honor. He moves over to Gerber and shakes his hand, wishes us both luck, and steps away while my mom hugs Gerber, a motherly move that she rightly believes my roommate needs. I offer to walk my parents to the car, but they tell me no, it's okay, I should settle in.

And then they're gone.

An hour later Gerber and I have unpacked. We head out of the dorm and meet up with Jimmy, his roommate, and a couple of guys on his floor. Before nightfall we've located a local off-campus bar that's famous for fifty-cent draft beers, cheap food, loose girls, and rocking out, and all I can say over and over to Jimmy and Gerber is, "This is unbelievable."

Freshman year challenges me. I struggle to juggle course work, swimming, and partying, often coming in at five a.m. wasted, vowing to take control of my life, to get my priorities straight, always ending up the next night back in a bar or at a party until five a.m. the following day. It's a pattern that I can't seem to break or, frankly, want to break. One day, I get up just before three in the afternoon, straggle into the bathroom, look at myself in the mirror, and stare at the unfamiliar face looking back at me. The guy resembles me, but with bloodshot and spacey eyes and a mop of hair in need of either a gallon of gel or a weed whacker. I lean into my reflection and say aloud, "You look like freaking *shit*. You gotta play this smarter or you're gonna burn out."

I take my own advice.

I get my priorities straight.

I quit the swim team.

I don't tell my dad.

I plan to drop the bombshell at home during Thanksgiving in the protection of extended family and what I know will be good-natured chaos around the table.

Meanwhile I puff out a sigh of relief. I can finally handle my schedule now that it's been reduced to partying every night and making an occasional appearance in class. Oh, yeah. Got college *wired*.

—

The banner sells me—enormous, twenty feet or more, draped between two bowing trees, nearly obscuring the front of the DK fraternity house: MOM AND DAD, GIVE US YOUR DAUGHTERS!

I imagine every parent of every freshman daughter issuing the same warning: "You are not allowed to go to that frat house," and every daughter thinking, *Soon as you leave, I'm going to that frat house.*

Fifty brothers in maroon-and-white T-shirts hoist half a dozen beer kegs over their heads like trophies won in battle, hollering at passersby, howling, roaring, plowed at five in the afternoon. They pour out of the house in a swarm, spilling onto the front lawn, standing on the swaying, dilapidated porch of their wreck of a house, to me the spitting image of Delta House in *National Lampoon's Animal House.* I stand outside during Rush Week and soak it all in, these guys, these maniacs, the pit they live in, and I know in the deepest part of me that I've found my home.

I rush, and along with Gerber and Jimmy Baxter, receive a bid. Gerber accepts his and becomes a DK pledge, but Jimmy and I turn ours down. I convince myself that I'm not ready for the commitment, but a part of me feels that if I pledge, I'll lose Jimmy. He's an artist, a musician, a nonconformist, and I can't see him accepting getting his ass paddled even if I'm bent over next to him getting mine whacked at the same time. So I turn down the bid. I regret it almost immediately because I realize that Jimmy and I have survived a worse separation when he moved away before middle school. I know our friendship is unconditional and that we'll survive my becoming a frat guy while he remains a civilian, and I really fucking want to be a DK.

Home for Thanksgiving, glowering beneath my new Travis Bickle Mohawk, my locks shorn in solidarity with Gerber and the other DK pledges even though I'm just watching from the sidelines, I send bored and superior death-ray stares across the table at my sisters, who barrage me with annoying questions, such as "How do you like college?" At some point I casually break the news that I've quit swimming and taken up rugby, a brutal sport that I enjoy because it combines three of my favorite activities: roughhousing with a ball, brawling, and non-stop drinking. My dad picks at his food slowly, nodding into his plate, not even pretending to hide his concern.

When I return to Geneseo for second semester, I find a letter in my mailbox with news from the house resident assistant, a guy I've run into maybe twice. I've been kicked out of the dorm. The reasons he gives are excessive partying and breaking dorm rules. I had no idea that I was breaking dorm rules or that our dorm even had rules. And I certainly didn't consider my partying *excessive*.

Thanks to a guy I know in DK, I find a room in an off-campus house owned by a creepy French literature professor I'll call Maurice, who routinely rents a few rooms to students. Maurice wears suits and speaks with an exaggerated French accent, which sounds fake, and sticks his nose in the air whenever he sees me, as if trying to locate the origin of a foul odor he's just detected. Maurice allows his tenants the run of his kitchen and common area but forbids us the use of his washer and dryer, a tremendous pain in the ass, since the closest Laundromat is several miles away and none of us has a car. Still, the living arrangement works, as long as I keep out of Maurice's way.

Sophomore year, I rush DK again. I'm told by Gerber and my buddy Bergie, my ins at the frat, that even though they'll push for me, the brothers didn't take kindly to my turning them down the first time, and a second bid may be a long shot. I rush hard and I know I'm on my game. The bid comes in. I pledge with the enthusiasm of a guts-and-glory Marine, a good thing since pledging DK is a lot like boot camp. At one point during Hell Night, downing some nauseating concoction blindfolded, I experience a strange realization, probably the result of having spent two days straight with no sleep and six weeks enduring mental manipulation that would make any professional interrogator proud: I am about to achieve one of the most important goals of my life.

I am about to become a brother.

———

Officially a DK, I invite my high school girlfriend, who goes to school in Albany, to spend the weekend with me in Maurice's house. We plan to attend a big party at the frat house Saturday night. Late Saturday afternoon, my girlfriend rummages in her suitcase, pulls out her outfit for the night, and heads for the washer and dryer. I explain that my landlord, the eccentric French lit professor, has banned the use of the washer and dryer. Then I check my watch. We don't have time to walk to town, do the laundry, and get back before the party. I decide to risk it, to break Maurice's rule just this once.

I shove her clothes into the washer, keeping my eyes and ears peeled for Maurice, then frantically remove the clothes when they're done and fling them into the dryer. Thirty minutes. That's all we need. As the clothes tumble and clang in the dryer, I start to pace. My girlfriend suggests that the time will pass quicker if I stop staring at the clothes. She grabs my hand and leads me outside for a walk.

When we get back, the dryer door is open and her clothes are gone.

"He is such a *freak*," I say. "Wait here."

I charge up the hill behind the house to the cottage where Maurice lives. I bang on the door and step back. The door swings open and Maurice stands defiantly in the doorway.

"*Oui?*" he says, sticking his nose up.

"You got my girlfriend's clothes," I say. "She needs them for tonight."

"That's a shame, because she's not having them. I told you that you cannot use the washer and dryer."

"I know you did, and I'm sorry. It won't happen again. Now can I please have her clothes?"

"No."

He starts to close the door. I shove my foot forward and block the door.

"Listen, let's cut this out," I say. "Just give me the clothes."

"I told you. *No.*"

"So you're gonna, what, steal her clothes?"

"You are calling me a thief? You broke the house rule."

"I know. Again, I'm sorry. Now, come on, please, give me her *clothes.*"

He sticks his nose even farther up in the air, then, with surprising speed, tries to push the door closed with both hands. I slam my shoulder into the door and force it back. Maurice's face burns hot, the color of a grape, his eyes narrow into slits, and he rushes me. He grabs me by my shirt and slams me against the inside wall of his cottage. I'm momentarily stunned. And then I glare at him. "Take your hands off me," I whisper.

I keep my arms at my side, my hands loose, my fingers splayed. I can feel his hands trembling in rage. He holds my shirt tighter, lifts me slightly, and then drops his hands.

"You have fifteen minutes to vacate my house," Maurice says.

"You're gonna regret this," I say.

I back up a few steps, head outside, find a pay phone, call the campus cops, and report Maurice.

Homeless now, I appeal to the brothers of DK. They have only one space available in the fraternity house, which they offer to me, a tiny room the guys call the Closet. I move in. They're wrong. A closet would be twice the size of this cranny. I can barely fit my bed in. I don't care. I feel as if I've moved home.

A few months later, I stand in a courtroom facing Maurice. Neither of us has brought a lawyer. I have, however, brought a dozen DK brothers who sit in the gallery, wearing blazers emblazoned with our fraternity's letters. The sea of support behind me boosts me as I present my case, and shakes up Maurice who stumbles through his recounting of "the incident," changing details to fit his claim that *I* put my hands on *him*.

In the end, the judge throws the case out, citing insufficient evidence and a waste of his time, a clear victory for me. The DKs lose it, hooting and cheering as if they're at a football game or standing around a craps table. On my way out of the courtroom, I slide past Maurice and glare at him. I want to grab him by the shirt now and get in his face and say, "Do not ever mess with me or the DKs, you dirtbag," but I keep my cool and walk out with my head high, feeling triumphant.

Second semester sophomore year, the DKs elect me recording secretary, a job that requires me to pay attention at board meetings and take notes, not two of my finer talents. Junior year I'm awarded the important position of house president, which differs radically from president of DK House, a prestige title, the face of DK, one I have my sights on for senior year. Being house president requires me to maintain the fraternity house, to clean it up and make it presentable, especially for parties. To be honest, keeping the DK house clean is a monumental task, almost as impossible as asking somebody to grow taller.

I throw myself into the job. I become a cleanliness freak, the Mr. Clean of Geneseo. I recruit pledges, but mostly I clean the horrific pit of a house myself. I carry hoses inside and wash down the entire first floor—living room, dining room, kitchen. I blast away with water at unidentifiable crud caked everywhere from countless years and fraternity parties. I pull on latex gloves and attack the most stomach-churning toilets in America, brushing, scrubbing, and scraping until the porcelain shines. I haul on rubber boots, the kind lobstermen wear, wade into the showers, and scrub and chip away at the scary and possibly alive black layer of goo crusted over the bathtub until the tile sparkles. At chapter meetings, I become the annoying fussy uncle, insisting that the brothers throw away their cups and plastic plates before they leave, sometimes snatching them right out of their hands. I take some cash from our emergency fund and rent a Dumpster, which I fill with dozens of plastic bags pregnant with garbage. The brothers observe my work ethic with a kind of reverence. Either they didn't think I had this in me or they've never seen anything quite like it. Truthfully, I surprised myself. But then I realize this is who I am. When I want something done, I go all in, with a passion.

"This is our house," I say. "It's our home. I want people to know that we're proud of this place. We may like to party, but we're not animals."

The brothers grunt like pigs, howl like monkeys, scratch themselves, and then they applaud.

———

Three of us wait in an upstairs bedroom.

We joke to cut the tension and then go silent, straining to listen through the floor, hearing mostly the beating of our own hearts. We are waiting for the results and we are nervous as hell.

We have all been nominated for president of the DKs.

One guy, call him Tony, says that he alone deserves the position. He feels entitled, believes it's his turn. The other guy, call him Ray, is a long shot and everybody knows it, especially Ray. Tony and Ray are both great guys. I'd throw myself in front of a bus for either of them, but I believe that I deserve the presidency more than they do.

Below us, in the chapter room, the heated voices of the DKs rise up and reach us through the floorboards. The brothers have taken sides and are discussing, debating, and then deciding who should lead the DKs. At one point, I hear a muffled voice say, "It's JT. He's the only one. I'm putting my onions on the line for him." Voices roar in agreement, then other voices shout those voices down.

Tony laughs. "You got no shot, JT," he says. "This is all mine."

"We'll see."

"I don't even know why I'm up here," Ray says. "Next year, maybe."

"No, man, you're worthy," I say. "The guys think highly of you. That's why they nominated you."

"Yeah, that, and they needed a third nominee," Tony says.

"Hey, Tone, if you don't get it, I think you'd be perfect for my job, house president," I say. "I can see you scrubbing the toilets, making them shine. I'll even gift you my latex gloves."

Ray snickers. Tony rolls his eyes, paces, and then someone knocks on the door. One of the brothers pokes his head in. "Okay, guys, come on down."

We walk into the chapter room and stand in the center of the membership, forty brothers strong who form a circle around us. The outgoing president steps in front of us. "All three of you are worthy candidates. But after much debate and discussion, we have decided. The next president of the DKs is"—he pauses and grins—"JT!"

The brothers erupt in applause and then they begin chanting. I feel light-headed, almost drunk, even though I haven't taken even a sip of beer. Hands surround me and push me forward and somehow Ray and Tony dissolve into the circle and then the circle tightens around me. The chanting fades and all forty of the brothers snap their fingers at once. Then there is silence. Now, for the first time, I address the DK brothers as their president.

"Thank you for this great honor," I say. "I will make you proud."

The brothers roar, a booming rumble that shakes the foundation and rises to the leaky roof of our dilapidated—but sparkling clean—house.

———

I wear my presidency like a favorite sweater: It's always *on*. I walk up to strangers on campus, especially girls, offer my hand, and introduce myself, "Hi, I'm JT, president of the DKs."

The DKs have officially elected me president, but I walk through Geneseo as if I'm still running for office.

I sense that I'm becoming *known*, particularly within the Greek world on campus. All frat guys seem to recognize me, even respect me. At parties I walk from room to room introducing myself, warmly greeting everyone. "Hi, I'm JT, president of the DKs" becomes my signature, my calling card, and I realize that JT has become my identity.

As senior year rolls on and my duties as president of DK intensify, I approach the office as a career, devote my spare time to rugby, and basically check out of all my classes. I stumble toward the finish line of graduation, barely crack the tape with enough credits to earn my diploma. I do graduate, though, and now, as I reflect, I realize that my time in Geneseo, my life with the DKs, both as a brother and as president, ultimately defined me. I may not have raised the bar academically, but in almost every other way I came into my own. With my dad as my role model, I prided myself on taking responsibility whenever I took on a job and on staying connected to my family, in this case my DK family. As a result, I earned my brothers' respect, and that meant more to me than anything.

I entered college a boy named John.

I graduated a young man named JT.

A week or so after the graduation ceremony, I stand outside the DK house wearing my cap and gown, my parents on either side of me. My dad lays an arm on my shoulder and says that he's proud of me for pulling this off, for graduating in four years as I promised. My mom nods at the DK house, swipes a tear that trickles down her cheek, and says, "I'm proud of you, too, and I can't believe that you actually lived in that pigsty."

"You should've seen it before I cleaned it up," I say.

Later that day I say good-bye to the people who have meant the most to me during my four years at Geneseo—my fraternity brothers, the guys on the rugby team, a couple of professors, and Gerber, who I know will remain a lifelong friend.

In the backseat of my parents' car, as we pull away from campus, I stare out the rear window, and through the gloomy gray sky I've become accustomed to every day for four years I watch the buildings of my college become smaller and smaller and then fade into the horizon. Moments from those four years flash into my mind, images in a loop—parties, rugby matches, pledging, being elected president, chapter meetings, evenings spent hanging out with my DK brothers. I think about college, gone in a blink, and I think about how I got through, what guided me, and what saved me.

Fate.

Driving away from Geneseo, the green hills of upstate New York enclosing us on either side, I realize that fate put me at the doorstep of the DK house and offered me the opportunity—the privilege—to pledge not once but twice. Fate kept at me. Fate saved my ass.

It will not be the last time.

3.

Just Give Me One Percent of Your Trust

Long Island and Connecticut
1987

THE YELLOW PAGES at my elbow, headset in place like air traffic control, I pound the phones, the script printed in boldface taped on the desk in front of me.

My goal:

Three hundred cold calls a day.

Twenty qualified prospects.

Ten new accounts a month.

Minimum.

I go for twenty.

Because I can.

I'm one of the few.

I prepare for battle.

I punch in the number.

My phone is my weapon.

My phone is my gun.

Today I call dry cleaners.

Two rings. A man answers. Broken English. Tone of annoyance. The loud hum of a pressing machine through the line threatening to drown him out.

"Mr. Sandoval, how are you doing? John Tournour from J.T. Moran. I know you're a busy man so I'm not gonna waste your time. I just want to ask you: If I found a stock that I believe will give you an exceptional rate of return, would you be interested? No? Are you sure? If I tell you that I'm positive I can open up a new account with you and get you fifteen to twenty percent return, minimum, how would you feel about that? Tell me, when you invest, what would be your typical investment? Five thousand dollars? Ten? Well, I'm certain I can find something for you. Do you mind if I call you back if I see something that will fit you? Excellent. Mr. Sandoval, give me one percent of your trust and I will *earn* the other ninety-nine percent. Great. Let's get the paperwork started. Take two minutes. May I have your Social Security number, please?"

On an index card, I write down phone numbers, business and home addresses, date of birth, Social Security number, and a time for me to drop by the cleaners and pick up his check.

Score.

I win.

No, I *dominate*.

I want to shout and pump my fist in the air, but I don't.

I trace the line of dry cleaners in the yellow pages with my finger and dial the next number.

My heart jumping, adrenaline pumping like it's the bottom of the ninth and I've come in to close, I pound the next call.

My two hundred thirteen call of the day.

I'm gonna fucking close this one, too.

I live for this.

—

One year earlier.

I'm living at home cutting lawns, taking job interviews, going nuts.

Rick, a guy I know from college, calls me out of the blue, tells me he's working at this place, J.T. Moran, and *killing* it, raking in serious cash and partying like every night's the weekend. He thinks I would fit right in. I'm outgoing, high energy, strong focus, a great talker, predicts I will take this job to another level, work the phones like a cold-call cowboy, and *sell*. Plus he knows I'll get along with everyone. They're our kind of guys, Rick says. Says it's like being back at Geneseo, in our fraternities. Rick invites me to an upcoming orientation. I hang up, realizing that Rick called to recruit me. I think, the guy's good.

—

A wide office space in the basement of a building. Couple of large offices to our right. A maze of cubicles to our left.

A boiler room.

Eight guys, all of us recent college grads, sit around a conference table. We tap pencils on legal pads, sip coffee from

Styrofoam cups, chug water from plastic bottles. We make small talk and wait. Everyone seems nervous, and I'm not sure why. I guess because we don't know what to expect and we feel vulnerable, like sitting ducks.

A door opens and a young guy, twenty-five tops, strides in. He wears a freshly pressed two-thousand-dollar suit, polished three-hundred-dollar shoes, a gelled hundred-dollar haircut slicked back, and a gleaming, terrifying smile. He holds that smile and skewers each one of us with it.

"Thanks for coming," he says. "I'm happy you're interested in J.T. Moran. The question is"—he tilts forward, presses his palms into the conference table—"are *we* interested in *you*?"

The eight of us squirm. A couple of us laugh uncomfortably. One guy coughs.

"But if we are, and if you can get through the rigorous screening process, which begins with taking two very tough tests, the series seven and the series sixty-three—by the way, you have to pay for that and the study materials and I'll need a check today—and *then* if we sponsor you, well, maybe, *maybe*, you can become a licensed stockbroker and crush it with J.T. Moran like my man Billy B., who started six months ago."

Billy B., a kid our age or slightly older, appears before us. Same suit, same shoes, same haircut, same razor smile.

"Billy," the first guy says, "how much you make last month?"

"Twelve grand," Billy says.

"And what car do you drive?"

"Brand-new 700 Beemer."

A parade of J.T. Moran brokers follows, one after another, as if they are male models, all dressed in uniform, ultrastylish, ultraexpensive suits, all claiming a monthly draw of ten grand or more, all driving Beemers, Porsches, or Benzes.

At some point, I drift off. I've been here before, not in this space, but in this mind-set, when I was president of the DKs, during Rush Week, when we wrangled every worthy undergraduate we could find, lured them all into our living room, and plied them with promises of the best parties on campus, famous for unlimited beer flow and nonstop, unbearably gorgeous and fuckable women. We sold the shit out of them. I'm sold now, sold by the suits, the salaries, and the cars, even though I know a dog and pony show when I see one.

I don't care.

I want this.

I want to be in this fraternity.

I want it bad.

—

Into year two at J.T. Moran, I'm pulling down six figures. I lease a 944 Porsche, maroon, because the colors of DK are maroon and white. I pay $495 a month. I buy a dozen suits. I ditch my old barber in favor of an expensive stylist.

At the company, my numbers soar. I lock in more qualified leads than anyone—twenty or more a month—consistently topping the leader board. I bounce into the office a warrior, every workday a war, my phone my invincible sword with which I bloody anyone who gets in my way. At night—almost every night—we carry our battle into our partying, competing for who can drink more, stay out later, get laid the most.

The end of every month brings a frenzy, all of us banging phone calls in our cubicles to meet our quota, many of us desperate, on the verge of melting down. Guys kick their chairs back and stand at their desks, shouting, pleading, sometimes collapsing in a hungover fog after a promising call ends in a hang-up. We are young and we live at a furious pace. We believe we can outrun anything.

I move up. I go from merely pushing dollar stocks, opening accounts, and collecting checks to running my own crew. While I continue cold-calling and *crushing* it, I become management, so-called. I train a team of my own, thirty young brokers, and receive a piece of their action. I become a model of the company's success, called upon to stride through the boiler room at orientation in *my* expensive suit, arrogantly describe *my* maroon 944 Porsche, watch the greenies lick their lips as I trumpet *my* monthly salary. I am a snake charmer in a roomful of wannabe snakes.

I recruit my cousin Geno, keep tabs on him and mentor him, and then move him and the rest of my team to Connecticut as part of the company's expansion. Living in a crash pad with Geno and another guy, I watch my lifestyle, both at work and at play, shift into another gear, revving up from the extreme to the excessive. As I overextend my workload, sometimes cold-calling into the evening and on weekends and partying like a rock star, I become aware, for the first time, of feeling stressed. I put on weight. Rather than exercising or watching my diet or cutting down on my drinking, I buy a dozen new suits a couple sizes larger. Instead of calling it a night at two or three a.m., I pull all-nighters and straggle into work looking and feeling like shit.

Still, my work ethic, my focus, and my storehouse of unlimited energy keep me well out in front of the other brokers, winning what I see as some kind of fucked-up race.

Then, weirdly, I feel something, almost like a persistent and unreachable itch. I can't put my finger on it at first, can't tell if it's an itch due to my out-of-control crazy lifestyle or the out-of-control nature of the company itself. Slowly I sense it, unmistakably, like a cool mist drifting in before a pelting downpour.

Trouble.

I see signs. A broker melting down in his car, sobbing, the car running, his hands frozen on the steering wheel, unable to turn off the ignition, unable to *move*. A client calling to cancel an account, telling me a stock that one of my team sold him is worthless and he's lost five thousand dollars he doesn't have and he can't pay this month's mortgage. A call from Jimmy Baxter— one of many—admitting that he's bored at his job in the city selling copiers but mainly he's worried about me. He talks about packing it in and moving to California, a fantasy we've shared for no less than ten years. But when he talks about it now, I can't connect. I seem distant, distracted, dazed, as if I've lost my way.

In fact, I have lost my way. I fell into J.T. Moran embracing the famous Gordon Gekko credo "Greed is good" and believing that the answer to the question always searing through me—What will make your dad proud?—was *money*. Earning a good living. Showing him I could make it on my own. He has preached to me often his two rules of success and of life: *Do the right thing* and *Stay away from losers*. I suddenly don't think I'm doing the right thing, and I'm elbow to elbow with losers all day long. And although I have no proof, no concrete evidence, I sense that the company itself is on the verge of burning up.

At the same time, I'm burning out.

One night I pull the Porsche into a long driveway leading to a mansion set in the rolling hills of a quaint, exclusive Connecticut town. I get out of my car and walk toward the house, which is rented by one of the senior brokers. The driveway looks like a car lot at a BMW and Porsche dealership. I wander inside feeling half-drunk even though I have yet to take a sip of anything stronger than water. The house is overrun with Moran brokers and their dates, or women they've collected for the evening. Music blares through the house, turning every room into a dance floor. I move from room to room in a kind of trance. Every room features cocktails and wine and finger food, and although I don't venture into the back bedrooms, I smell weed and hear rumors of cocaine. I drift to the back of the house, walk outside through French doors toward the pale blue of an Olympic-size swimming pool, the same sort of pool in which I spent half my life. Now half-naked women and men splash and frolic and make out. I feel like I'm standing at the edge of some ridiculous Hollywood orgy. As I go back inside, I watch brokers and their dates, drunk or stoned—or drunk *and* stoned—leave the party, head to the driveway and their overpriced rides, lost in their overextended lives.

Everything about this party feels foreign yet numbingly familiar. It is every party and it is the same party. It is a party as a war zone with young warrior brokers trying to outdrink, outfuck, and outlast one another. At twenty-four, I'm not only a veteran of these wars, I'm over the hill. I pour myself a drink, bring it to my mouth, stop, stare inside the glass, and put it down. I ease my way into the front hallway and wait outside the locked bathroom. In a few minutes, the door opens and a broker and a hard-looking twenty-three-year old in a tight miniskirt that must make it hard for her to breathe come out laughing, running fingers along their gums. I slip inside the bathroom and lock myself in. I stare at myself in the mirror.

I look forty.

Ruddy, loose flesh. Thin, dry mouth. Hollowed-out vacant eyes that can't blink.

I lean my hands on the basin and feel them tremble.

I know that I have come to the end.

4.

Birth of the Brick

I PACK LIGHT, filling a suitcase and a backpack with everything I'll need for the rest of my life—underwear, socks, shorts, swimming trunks, T-shirts, jeans, a couple of dress shirts, a tie, and a suit. I grab toiletries, a few books, my baseball glove, and the small clock radio that sits on my nightstand. I leave all of my winter clothes behind.

We head out on a Friday morning before dawn, under the cover of darkness. Jimmy parks his van in the driveway and I shove my stuff into the back, pushing my suitcase through the cheap dense shag carpeting and tossing in my backpack so it rests against one of the two captain's chairs Jimmy has installed. In addition to laying carpeting on the floor and on the walls, scavenging the chairs from a flea market, and buying and stocking a cooler, Jimmy has tricked the van out with a sound system designed to blow our heads off. I'm stoked. I think the van looks like a bachelor pad on wheels. In later years, I'll reassess and decide that it more accurately resembled a set in a porno film.

For weeks, I'd talked with my parents about moving to California. My mom, as usual, tamped down her concern and expressed mostly quiet support. My dad, who encouraged me to bail from J.T. Moran once he, too, saw that the firm was about to go belly-up, wanted to know my plan, assuming that I had a plan. He needed to know where I was going and what I would do.

"Got it covered, Dad," I told him. "We're going to San Diego and I've lined up a job at Smith Barney."

"Why San Diego?" my mother asked. I think for both of them San Diego seemed like a mysterious, exotic locale at the far end of the Earth.

"L.A.'s too crazy, San Francisco's too cold. San Diego is America's finest city." I wasn't sure how I'd come to that claim, probably from something I'd read in a magazine in the dentist's office. It didn't really matter because Jimmy and I had done our own research, consisting of compiling maps and considering locations, all in warm weather locales, conferring with our friends and my fraternity brothers who'd relocated west, and watching the Padres and Chargers on TV and admiring the stunningly blue skies, palm trees, and flimsily clad women whenever the camera panned the stadium. We wanted no more of East Coast winters or jobs that crushed our spirits. We wanted to start over. We wanted California.

"California," my mother said. "It's so—"

"Far?" I said.

"I was going to say *different*."

And then we came to the day. A couple days before, Jimmy had hesitated, wondering if we should put off heading out until Monday, but I dug in. "We've been planning this for weeks. Let's get out of here. Let's go. We gotta cut the cord, man."

The night before our departure, I write my parents a letter, my thoughts rambling over several pages on a legal pad. I know the move must be tearing at them both. I write to thank them for letting me go without standing in my way and I thank them for being extraordinary parents. I apologize for being a challenge at times, for being the cause of most of their gray hairs, for not meeting what I know to be—especially for my dad—their high expectations, and for being less than a perfect brother to my younger sisters. I tell them that I have to do this; I have to go out on my own, find my own way, figure out who I am. I thank them for understanding that. As I write, the words flowing furiously, I start to cry. What I don't say—what I can't say—is what I know to be the deepest truth.

I am writing to say good-bye.

I don't know how I know this, I just do.

I know that I am moving to California and that I am never coming back.

I put down my pen and sob.

An hour later, drained and racked with guilt, I finish the letter. I sign my name, fold it, and place it on my dad's desk.

And then I am gone.

We take the southern route. We stop first in D.C., stay with a couple of DKs, and party hard in Georgetown. Then we swing down to South Carolina and hang with a fraternity brother who's joined the army and is stationed at Fort Jackson, where we learn that army guys like to let loose. Next on to New Orleans and nights of insanity on Bourbon Street. We bomb from Bourbon Street all the way, in one shot, white-line fever, to Austin, Texas, where we hole up in a cheap hotel near Sixth Street. We get into the Austin music and bar scene like champions and stay longer than we planned. We haul ass through New Mexico, stop outside of Phoenix, and hit the Salt River Water Park in Mesa, where we throw on our bathing suits, get drunk, soak up the sun, and go tubing. A few hours later, dried off, dried out, washed out, wasted, and stuck on a one-lane highway in bumper-to-bumper traffic that refuses to budge, I take my turn to drive while Jimmy conks out in one of the captain's chairs. After fifteen minutes of moving approximately one inch, feeling exhausted and frustrated, I slump my head onto the steering wheel. I turn slightly and catch a glimpse of Jimmy sacked out beneath a blanket up to his chin, a beatific smile snaked across his face, and I lose it.

"I'm done," I say, snapping my head up, speaking through the windshield toward the road. "I'm done with this driving shit."

I slam the van into park.

The move jars Jimmy. He lowers the blanket, blinks, and squints at me. "What?"

"I'm fucking *done*."

I climb into the back and sack out in the other captain's chair. I wrestle the blanket away from Jimmy and cover myself.

"What are you doing?" he says. "It's your turn to drive."

"I'm not driving anymore. I'm sick of it."

"You can't stop here!"

"I just did."

A car horn blares. Then another. Then a third.

"Fuck you, cars," I say, tipping the visor of my Yankees cap over my eyes, squirming in the chair, trying to get comfortable.

"Get up there and drive," Jimmy says.

"Nope."

"You *asshole*," Jimmy hollers, but he's half laughing.

"Whatever."

"Drive!"

Jimmy begins pelting me with a torrent of stuff, some of which I can identify by its feel—a newspaper, a magazine, an empty soda can, a drumstick we picked up in Austin, a wet bathing suit, and a barrage of half-empty puke-smelling take-out food containers from as far away and long ago as Georgetown.

The chorus of horns bleats behind us.

"Fuck me," Jimmy says.

I hear his chair creak as he climbs out, feel him step over me and wham me in the ribs, and hear him groan as he lands in the driver's seat. After a moment, I feel the van lurch forward.

"Shit, man, take it easy," I say. "I'm hungover."

Something harder nails me in the head and knocks off my Yankees cap. I mumble, "Ouch," add, "You suck," and nod off.

Two days later, at sunset, thirty-six hours before I'm to begin my stockbroker career at Smith Barney in downtown San Diego, we hit Mission Beach. Jimmy, at the wheel, eases over to the shoulder of Mission Boulevard and stops the van. I stare at the Pacific Ocean, the waves calmly lapping onto the shoreline of the whitest sand I've ever seen.

"We made it," Jimmy says, his voice quiet, subdued, as if he'd been harboring serious doubt that we'd ever get here.

"Wow," I say. I push open the passenger door and step out of the van. I kick off my shoes and step onto the beach. I walk toward the water, then break into a jog. I pull up ten feet before the waves break. A second later, I feel Jimmy next to me. I keep staring straight ahead into the Pacific, riveted by the sun, an orange blot bobbing on the horizon, about to sink into the sea.

"We're here," I say. "We're in California."

And then, unexpectedly, because I'm overcome by the sheer beauty of the muted orange sunlight spreading over the Pacific Ocean, or feeling small and lost, or shaken that I've left my previous life 3,000 miles away, or I'm having my first truly religious experience, I drop to my knees and crash onto the white sand. My entire body pulses with exhilaration and promise and I lift my arms toward the plunging orange sun and I scream Jimmy's words, *We made it!*

Three months later.

The San Diego yellow pages at my elbow, headset strapped on, the boldfaced script taped in a neat square on my desk, I pound the phones.

My goal:

Three hundred cold calls a day.

Twenty qualified prospects.

Ten new accounts a month.

I circle a plumbing company in red, breathe, and stifle a yawn that sneaks up and surprises me. I shake it off. My hand reaches forward. My fingers dangle above the number pad, preparing to pounce, and...

I hesitate.

And then I freeze.

I breathe again and lower my hand, realizing—

I can't pull the trigger.

I swallow the lump of panic that has bubbled into my throat.

From my cubicle, I survey the bull pen, a mass of suited stockbrokers banging phone calls, the hum of their voices building to a roar that sticks in the cloud that has floated into my mind. I spot Tim Cusick—the guy I cold-called from New York and asked for a job out of the blue and who to my astonishment hired me and set me up with a six-month draw—standing outside his office in conversation with two other guys, Jerry, the big boss, a stern, strict, by-the-numbers guy, and a brand-new broker, a kid right out of college, green and eager. I can't read lips but I imagine Jerry is fielding a question about some wrinkle in the new bond fund we discussed first thing this morning in a meeting I nearly missed because I came in twenty minutes late. Jerry, who was leading the meeting, didn't say anything when I walked in tucked into a slight crouch, trying to sneak into a seat in the back, but I saw a clear look of annoyance drift across his face like a shadow. I had my excuse ready, something lame about the traffic, even though I knew I was on shaky ground since there is no traffic at six a.m., the time Jerry called the meeting. That's the first hurdle I'm trying to get over out here. The time difference. The market opens at nine thirty a.m. on the East Coast, a reasonable hour, but six thirty in San Diego, an ungodly hour. As the partying at our apartment normally goes deep into the early morning, rarely heating up until one or two, I'm lucky to catch three hours of sleep before I have to hit the shower, suit up, and make it to the office by six thirty, six if we have a meeting.

As for landing in the right city in America, Jimmy and I nailed it. San Diego rules. Summer weather 24/7, book-ended by gentle breezes blowing through every morning and evening to cool us down. Every day is the same, no vicious weather to deal with, no sign of the seasons. You tell me it's winter, I have to take your word.

After spending the first few nights on a friend's couch and floor, Jimmy and I rent a two-bedroom, two-bath apartment on the beach. We call it Club E309. We have everything two transplanted New Yorkers committed to partying could ever want or need: the world's whitest, softest, sandiest beach outside our back door; a private patio for barbecuing; swimming pool; Jacuzzi; community hot tub constantly stocked with half-naked women toting pitchers of beer; two awesome bars on the beach just footsteps away, each offering a vibrant singles scene; and a nonstop parade of girls in bikinis Rollerblading past, checking us out, and we them, later joining us for beach volleyball, bodysurfing, sunbathing, beer pong, chilling, and then drinks, dinner, and whatever may happen later. Paradise. At our doorstep.

Soon after settling in, I arrange to have my dad send me my Porsche. Once my car arrives, I call the boys from back east, the ones we left behind—Krebs, the Rocket Man, and the Home Wrecker—and give them the word: "The Eagle has landed. Get out here, boys." And so they do. In a matter of weeks they descend with suitcases and backpacks and we create DK West, only wilder, because we have no restrictions, no classes, and no one to answer to. One night, sitting at a table at Billy Bones, one of our go-to bars, watching two teams of near-naked women go at each other in a sweaty, sexy game of beach volleyball, I tip my beer bottle at the horizon and say, "This is it, boys. This is why we came out here. This is why I left."

"For the girls," someone says.

"Nope." I shake my head, take a long drink, lower my bottle, and lean its cool neck against my forehead. "For the freedom."

—

My panic swallowed, snaking back down into a bitter thread in my stomach, I study the phone in front of me. The instrument looks strangely distant, and then unfamiliar, and then before my eyes, the phone shrinks, becoming smaller and smaller until it's the size of a child's fist. I blink, polish my forehead with my palm and feel throbbing, unexpected heat. I push back in my chair. *I need to get a fucking grip.* I'm afraid suddenly that I've been stricken with alcohol poisoning, or I'm hallucinating because of my severe lack of sleep and that my insane partying has lopped off a piece of my mind. I swear to cut down on my drinking and curtail the partying. I mutter to nobody in particular to please shake me out of this. I just want to do my job, return to my glory as Cold-Call King. I reach for the tiny distant phone, and as if drawn by a magnet my hand slams back to my side.

I realize then that I'm suffering from a condition worse than alcohol abuse or sleep deprivation, a disease that threatens to ravage my very core.

Disillusionment.

I'm through being a stockbroker.

I can't make three hundred cold calls.

I can't find twenty qualified leads or open ten new accounts.

I can't do this anymore.

Three more months of money coming in.

That's all I have left.

But in truth I have nothing left.

Because I'm done.

———

Driving home from Smith Barney one afternoon, I pull over to the side of the road, pick up the mobile phone in my car, and make my second call ever to sports talk radio.

I call Lee "Hacksaw" Hamilton, venerable sports talk host on San Diego's Mighty 690. Lee is railing about the lack of fan support for the Padres while certain community leaders are trying to push through funding for a new stadium. Lee's asking for listeners' opinions. I want in. I have something to say.

As I wait on hold, I remember the first phone call I made to sports talk radio, a year ago at least, a forgettable twenty-second exchange with New York sports talk legends Mike and the Mad Dog. One Friday afternoon, home for the weekend, bored, lying in bed, listening to the two hosts hollering at each other about the Giants or the Knicks, their voices slightly muffled through my small clock radio, I grabbed the phone and called in. Before I knew it, I was on the air, and seconds after I spoke, I felt crushed between Mike's authoritative bass and Mad Dog's manic, shrill tenor. I held on to the phone long after they ended the call and thought, *That was a waste. I'll never do that again. Even though I know I can do better.* I kept tuning in to them until the moment Jimmy and I left, and although I forgot about that call, my mind too focused and blotto during each adventure that unfolded by the minute in the course of our epic cross-country trip, some kind of itch remained.

As I wait by the side of the road, an occasional truck rumbling past and shaking the car, Hacksaw's voice reverberates through the radio in the Porsche and then, jarring me, says, "Let's go to JT in San Diego. What's on your mind?"

I click off the radio as his producer has instructed and hear myself talk through the mobile phone about arriving here recently from New York a Yankees fan, going to Yankee Stadium with my dad, and watching some of the best players of all time. I say that I've gone to the ballpark here several times to see Tony Gwynn, who ranks with the best of them, a future Hall of Famer, one of the purest hitters to ever live. I implore Padres fans to get out to the ballpark and see this guy play. If they don't, I say, they're missing out on witnessing greatness right in their own backyard.

Hacksaw agrees with me, thanks me for the call, lets me go, and trots out a bunch of Tony Gwynn's stats to prove my point.

In the car, with Hacksaw bleating through the radio, I lean back in the driver's seat. I feel the way I did when I was younger and swimming mattered and I'd lift myself out of the pool after beating a better swimmer in a race I wasn't supposed to win.

I feel pumped.

My six months at Smith Barney are coming to an end. My draw is running out, my prospects running dry, my enthusiasm nonexistent, my tardiness continual and unmanageable. I can feel Jerry, the big boss, eyeing me with disgust as if I'm roadkill. I get a call one day from Charles Singer, a friend of a client and a partner at Sperry Van Ness, a high-end commercial real estate company in the area. Charles, rude, raw, hilarious, and extremely British, throws me a lifeline.

"Come on over," he says.

"Real estate? I don't know," I say, even though I'm so out the door at Smith Barney that anything above driving a Good Humor truck sounds promising.

"Now's the time," Charles says. "Look, if you have as much energy as I've been told and you're not afraid to cold-call people out of the blue, you'll do extremely well in real estate."

"You have no idea," I say. "Cold-calling is my game."

Charles pauses and whispers for effect. "Did I mention I'll greatly increase the commission you get now?"

"What time does the workday start?" I say. "I have to come in here in at six thirty in the morning."

"That's bloody *awful*. Inhumane. You're not on the clock with me. You make your own hours."

I resign from Smith Barney that afternoon.

⌒

We pack up DK West, Jimmy settles into his own place, and the Home Wrecker and I relocate to upscale La Jolla, where Sperry Van Ness has opened its main office. Saddened by the loss of our go-to bars on the beach and especially the onslaught of nubile Rollerblading females, we scope out La Jolla in search of replacements for both. We turn the corner from our apartment and our jaws drop. La Jolla features a bar every ten feet populated by hot, available young women. The nonstop party continues.

At work, I hit the ground running. I study for my real estate license, lock that in, and, under Charles's tutelage, start cold-calling. My goal now is to locate the owners of office buildings and apartment complexes who would consider selling their properties and giving us their listings. Even though I'm working without a draw, meaning I have no actual money coming in, I'm convinced that it's only a matter of time before I start making a killing in commercial real estate in California, the way my boss has.

"Real estate . . . ," my dad says when I tell him I've switched jobs, his voice trailing off.

"It's where it's at out here, Dad. Much bigger upside."

"Uh-huh. What happened with Smith Barney?"

"My time ran out there. To be honest, it wasn't a perfect fit."

My dad pauses. I can almost hear his mind sifting through a basket of words, choosing the right ones to say. "Well, it sounds like you got it under control," he says finally, and adds, "Good."

"Yeah, I do. Thanks."

Of course, I have nothing under control, not even close, and after we hang up, in a moment of weakness, I consider calling my dad back and asking for a loan. I recently went through an assessment of my finances and, bottom line, I have a lot more going out than coming in. While I have saved some money, mainly from the days at J.T. Moran, paying my bills every month will be a stretch until my real estate commissions start kicking in. I don't mention my shaky financial state to my dad, but he must sense something, because before the month ends a check arrives in the mail for $495, the exact amount of my car payment.

Every morning, with newfound focus and energy, I hit the pavement at seven a.m. and scour the streets of North San Diego following the maps in my dog-eared *Thomas Guide*, its pages swelling, tearing, and popping out of the cheap metal rings that try to enclose them. I'm in search of apartment buildings of one hundred units or more, what we call likely suspects. When I find one, I camp out across the street and then roam around the back and side of the building and snap a series of photos like I'm a paparazzo. I return to the office as soon as I'm finished with the day's photo shoot and, with Charles's help, create a "book," an album of properties with my snap-shots, descriptions I write, and research I include—owner, date and amount of the building's last sale, comparable listings, and an estimate of today's market value. My book grows thick as a dictionary. After months of seven a.m. mornings shooting pho-tos and compiling lists of properties, Charles puts me on the phones. Back to my comfort zone. Cold-calling.

My goal:

Three hundred calls a day.

Twenty legitimate leads.

The usual.

I'm the newest real estate broker in the room.

And when it comes to cold calls, I'm on fire.

I smoke the next closest guy.

———

A new restaurant scene explodes on the Aventine in La Jolla. Asian fusion. New-Age Mexican. Small plates Italian. And each new restaurant offers up a scalding hot new bar blowing funk or rap or salsa or classic rock, with neon lighting throbbing through the decor. Most weeknights and every weekend I round up my old guys and connect them with my new crew, guys I've met at Sperry Van Ness and around town—led by bachelor number one, Bobby G.—and we hit the bars and restaurants on the Aventine in a fast and furious brotherhood of twenty guys, who, after hard days of pushing hot properties, enter the premises in full force, thirsty and horny. Romantically, I shake it up, drifting from one-night stands to women I'm on the verge of dating long-term. But in the early mornings, after they all leave, before I face the day, two separate but equal truths shoot through me like sudden jolts of electricity:

1. I feel as if I'm still a wild twenty-one-year-old living in the DK house, where my whole life is one continuous epic party. But I'm *not* twenty-one, and I'm not in college anymore. I'm an adult. Allegedly.

2. I've been busting my ass compiling books of apartment buildings and cold-calling like a crazed maniac for almost two years and I've yet to make a dime in commercial real estate.

Then, in 1994, a third truth hits.

Commercial real estate in California crashes.

Analysts calculate that the value of all commercial property plummets more than 30 percent.

The reality of making a killing in real estate is now dead.

One day, Charles takes me to lunch. We order drinks. Charles folds his hands on top of his menu and nods once. "You need to get out," he says.

I rub my palm over my menu, pick it up, and pretend to look at it.

"I don't know when this market is going to turn around," he says. "No one does. It could take years. If you try to wait it out, you'll deplete any savings you have and you'll end up moving back home. I don't think that's what you want."

I say nothing.

"I've taken the liberty of making a call to a friend of mine who runs the Merrill Lynch office in La Jolla. He's offering you a desk and a small salary to start. The kicker is he wants you to play on the company softball team. I'd jump at it."

I lower the menu and look at him. "Back to selling stocks," I say. "Cold-calling clients."

"It's what you know," Charles says.

I stare out the window and watch the noon sunlight skimming off the metal of passing cars.

"He's waiting for your call," Charles says.

"I don't know if I can do that anymore, Charles," I say.

"Well, what else can you do?"

—

Running on fumes, blotto from partying, my savings account balance dipping toward empty, my soul ravaged, I sit in my cubicle at Merrill Lynch and fasten my headset. I flip open the yellow pages and stare at boldface columns of likely suspects. I have a job to do. I have a quota to meet.

My goal:

Three hundred cold calls a day.

One hundred potential clients.

Twenty qualified leads.

Ten new accounts a month.

Impossible?

No.

I *crush* it.

Every day.

How?

I have no idea.

Nobody has any clue that I have checked out and how close to zero I feel. But somehow I arrive at work on time every day and my adrenaline kicks in or my competitive juices flow and I hit those phone lines *hard*. Harder than anybody else. But I know I'm flaming out.

I don't know how long I can keep going before I run out of money. Or out of time. Or I lose my mind.

———

Jim Rome is huge and he has thousands of clones.

That's what he calls the members of his radio audience who make up his hard-core listening base. He paints a picture of jobless losers and stoners living at home or in shabby basement apartments where they do nothing all day except geek out on video games and tune in to his radio program, which he calls *The Jungle*.

Recently, Rome has exploded onto the sports talk radio scene, outdistancing Hacksaw and all the other hosts on San Diego's Mighty 690. Rome invites his audience to call in, but he warns them to "have a take" and "to not suck." He will unceremoniously hang up on and deride those callers who add nothing to the show. Rome speaks in colorful surfer slang, creating an exclusive vocabulary he calls smack, a language that you cannot possibly understand unless you listen to him every day.

I listen to him every day.

I'm hooked.

But I am not a clone. I have a job and a life. And responsibilities, including my current, most important position—outfield or third base on the Merrill Lynch softball team. I excel at softball. I am the ringer the team recruited in the off-season, the player other teams fear. I catch anything that comes my way and I'm a monster at the plate. We cruise into the league championship game and win easily. But while softball distracts me, it doesn't drive me. Softball doesn't get me through the day.

Sports talk radio does.

And specifically, Jim Rome.

But I am *not* a clone.

I am, however, a caller.

And I do not suck.

—

The hosts call me JT from La Jolla.

I call randomly at first, a few times to Hacksaw, a few more to Steve Hartman and Chet Forte, known as the Loose Cannons. I pick up the pace until I'm a regular caller, averaging a call a week. I call from home, the new apartment I share with the Home Wrecker, holed up in my bedroom that came furnished with bunk beds; I call from the mobile phone in my Porsche, officially *mine*, thanks to my dad; and, with my small clock radio a fixture now on my desk at Merrill Lynch, I call from work. I call sports talk radio shows while I make cold calls, flipping back and forth between the red blinking lights of potential clients and sports talk radio producers, keeping one eye on the yellow pages while shuffling index cards I aim to complete with pertinent information I've finagled out of my qualified leads, and the other on the lookout for the newly arrived big boss, Jerry, the same stern by-the-numbers Jerry who considered me a step above roadkill when we both worked at Smith Barney. He's come with a mission: get this office to produce and root out the brokers who aren't pulling their weight. I keep a vigilant eye on Jerry because I know he's watching me.

Eventually I put all of my energy and all of my heart into Rome.

I don't merely listen to his show, I study it. I don't realize what I'm doing at first, but I soon discover that I'm analyzing the structure and flow of his show, trying to break it down. I determine that Rome really doesn't want callers on his show. He wants *characters*. Most of Rome's best callers bring a Southern California color into *The Jungle*, variations of laid-back surfer dudes. To counter that, I create a new persona: JT from New York, a caller in love with the Giants, Yankees, and, especially, the Knicks. I call Rome with a blast of New York City energy, edge, and passion. I approach my phone calls as a *fan*. I'm the opposite of a stat freak or sports history dork. I'm a regular guy with a nine-to-five job who goes to games whenever he can and cheers his ass off for the home team. I praise the swagger of John Starks, the muscle of Anthony Mason, the drive of Patrick Ewing. I call out the Chicago Bulls and our nemesis, Michael Jordan, saying that this year we'll steam into the play-offs behind our slick-haired fashion-plate coach, Pat Riley.

I call frequently and soon I call Rome exclusively. I call when the spirit moves me, which means when I know I have a strong, funny take to bring into *The Jungle*. The spirit moves me often because I spend much of my time at home and at work thinking about my next call to Rome. I don't write anything down. When I'm ready, I call in, exchange a few words with his producer, Joe Tutino, and wait on hold until Jim is ready to take my call. When he does, I roar my New York fan "take" in a kind of inspired improvisation, ending in hopes that he will tell his producer to "rack" me, making me eligible to win the "huge call of the day," which I do, more than occasionally. Each call goes as long as a minute, and sometimes longer. One time I call insisting that the Knicks will go deep into the play-offs against the Bulls because I've analyzed both teams and I think the Knicks have the deeper, more talented roster.

"Pippin's not that great," I rant. "Their bench is weak...," and I'm off, the ultimate Knicks fan fomenting from the mouth.

When I finish, Rome chuckles and refers to me as "JT the *Brick*, from La Jolla," *Brick* being part of smack lexicon, his term for the Knicks. When I make my next call to Rome a few days later, he introduces me simply as JT the Brick.

And I am born.

5.

King of Smack

San Diego
April 26, 1995
Good Friday

JIM ROME GIVES me a way out.

Rome announces that, on Good Friday, two weeks away, he will devote his entire show to what he calls the First Annual Great American Smack-Off, an invitation-only contest in which he will determine the best caller of the year. The winner will receive his own phone line, a separate number on which he may call in at any time, jumping ahead of all the other callers who are waiting on hold, often for longer than an hour. Even cooler, the winner will be crowned the King of Smack and will appear with Rome himself at three different "tour stops"—remote broadcasts—in three separate Southern California locations. Over time, Rome's Smack-Off will become one of the most popular features in the history of sports talk radio.

Sitting in my cubicle at Merrill Lynch, my ear lowered toward my clock radio, I hear Jim Rome invite twenty contestants, including me—JT the Brick—to compete in the Smack-Off.

I push back in my chair and say softly, "This is it."

In fact, I can't articulate what *it* actually *is*, but I know with every ounce of my being that I have to win the Great American Smack-Off. I know that for me this is more than a contest for callers to a radio show. And I know, beyond a doubt, that I have been preparing for this contest my entire life.

It's a phone competition, I think. *Are you kidding? Who is better on the phone than me? Nobody can beat me.*

For the next two weeks, I let everything else slide—work, girlfriend, social life—and focus on nothing but the Smack-Off. I have never written notes for a phone call, never tried to write down funny lines or key points. But this is different. I'm leaving nothing to chance. I vow to be rested and prepared. This one time I decide to take notes and refer to them during the call. The night before the contest I blow off hitting the bars with Bobby G., Jimmy B., and the Home Wrecker. I stay in the apartment, sit at my desk, nurse a beer, and scribble bullet points that flow onto three pages of a legal pad. I don't rehearse what I'm going to say, but I look over the points I've written and refine them, revise them, reorder them, and punch them up. I go to bed satisfied that I'm ready, having finished only half the beer.

Friday morning I pull the Porsche into the Merrill Lynch parking lot. As I find a space close to the entrance, I realize that there are no other cars in the lot. The office has closed for

Good Friday. I unlock the door and enter the deserted office space. I stride over to my cubicle, clear my desk, and tape down my three pages of handwritten notes. I tape them in front of me in the same place I tape my script for cold-calling clients. But today I'm not trying to get strangers to purchase shares in Whoop-Dee-Do Industries or Useless Swampland Incorporated. Instead I'm about to put everything on the line—my reputation as a caller, my cold-calling talent, my *onions*, and, although I don't want to face it or say it aloud, my future.

I line the edges of my pieces of paper with a second layer of tape. I don't want my notes to crinkle when I'm on the air or accidentally fly away. I check the time. I click on the clock radio. Rome's theme song, "Welcome to the Jungle," comes on. I fold my hands in front of me and breathe slowly. I feel calm and I feel powerful.

I bide my time. I don't want to call too soon and risk getting lost in the early calls. But I can't call too late and chance that I'll be shut out.

I listen for an hour. The calls seem weak. Rome agrees. He complains about the surprising lack of quality *smack* from the Smack-Off contestants. He sounds worried that what he'd envisioned as an annual event may turn out to be a bust. I exhale, clear my throat loud enough for the sound to echo through the empty bull pen. It's time. I dial the phone. Joe Tutino, Rome's producer, acknowledges me and then puts me on hold.

After only a few minutes, Tutino comes on the line and tells me that I'm up next. He asks if I'm ready. I allow myself a quiet chuckle.

"I'm more than ready," I tell him.

He clicks off and puts me back on hold. An odd feeling comes over me, something that I can't immediately place. I can only identify it as a feeling of Zen. I no longer feel powerful. I feel untouchable.

And then I hear Rome's voice in my headset. He speaks with more urgency than I feel. He introduces me.

I edge forward in my chair and the charge inside me ignites.

Van Smack, what an honor to be a part of the First Annual Great American Smack-Off. Today proves there are few Tarzans in the Jungle. The rest are a bunch of Cheetah chimps who wished they had game like me...

A fresh burst of energy kicks in and I'm roaring.

But don't forget where my loyalty lies. The greatest city, the greatest tradition, the best smack comes from New York and the Bricks. When the earthquake hit, I didn't pick up the fish wrap to read about the damage. I looked at the box scores to see if the Knicks pulled out another gutty win. I have a passion to see Cal Ripken rupture a kidney this season rather than see him break my beloved Lou Gehrig's record.

When the baseball strike went down, I didn't feel for the working stiff whose only job is to mop up the bathroom floor after I missed the urinal. Who cares about the seventy-year-old grandma who serves beer at a pathetically slow pace so I have to miss two full innings of baseball?

When the Rangers won the Stanley Cup after fifty-four years, you have no idea how I felt. It's a passion. It's my life.

Today is a celebration of smack. I compare my experience to pledging my fraternity in college. For the first few months, I was a punk who had to wait on hold and pick and choose my spots to smack. Now

I feel like the pledge master who gets to spank the new plebes on the butt while they say, "Thank you, JT the Brick, can I please have another?"

Rome pauses and then says, "Was there any doubt about the Brick? That was an *epic* blast. That ball is still traveling, and it might not come down for days."

More callers follow but they should've stayed home.

I win the contest going away.

I am the King of Smack.

After the contest, Joe Tutino calls me back and makes it official. He congratulates me and tells me to wait on hold. Rome replays my winning call and then speaks to me on the air. I bounce to my feet in my cubicle and survey the silent Merrill Lynch office that lies vacant before me like a scene in an apocalyptic movie. Suddenly the calm that had overtaken me evaporates. I start to sweat and my body tingles with adrenaline. I want to put my head down and sprint through the empty office. I feel as if I could run a one-minute mile.

"Brick, phenomenal effort," Rome says.

"A *monster* win," I say, the words feeling trapped in my throat. For a moment, I don't recognize my own voice, then I roar, "Van Smack, I am fired up. When you win the first of anything, it's big. Hopefully, my smack will hold up in years to come."

"Brick, you stepped up. You are the King of Smack. Never again do you have to wait on hold. Write down this phone number. Commit it to memory."

He announces the number and I grab a red marker and scribble the digits in the top margin above my notes, circling the numbers in a manic series of red rings.

"I'll remember this more than my own phone number, my address, or my Social Security number," I say.

"Excellent, Brick. An omnipotent scud. Party now with the Bricks. You earned it."

"Thanks, Van Smack. The Bricks are en route…"

The rest of the conversation—the rest of the day and night—dissolves into a blurry montage. I pack up for the day, lock the outside door to the office, and walk to my car in a trance. I feel as if I'm floating above the pavement. My head spinning, feeling high, I drive to our apartment, less than five minutes away, and when I pull in front of the building, H., visiting from Massapequa, Jimmy B., Bobby G., the Home Wrecker, all waiting outside, shouting and hoisting beers, charge me and surround me. They pummel me, pound me, tousle my hair, and then someone slams a cold bottle of beer into my palm. They never listen to sports talk radio, none of them, but today they all listened, and they all heard.

"The King of *Smack*," someone shouts.

"JT the *Brick*!" a voice from inside the apartment screams as I stumble inside, my boys at my back. Chords of classic rock from the band Rush blast through the bass-heavy speakers in our living room and I break into a clumsy dance move, and then my girlfriend of the moment opens her arms, swoops in, and kisses me with beery lips, and then I'm laughing and dancing and more people arrive, an army armed with coolers of booze and beer and wings and snacks and pizza, and soon the air in the apartment reeks of beer and popcorn and pepperoni and sweat, but mostly the place smells of winning—yes, the place reeks of fucking *winning*—and three thirty that Good Friday afternoon, the all-night celebration begins, and in some sense it never stops.

And that smell of winning?

I never want that to fade.

I vow to wear that smell forever.

———

A week later, holding court at the National Sports Grill, a popular sports bar in Anaheim, Jim Rome looks over the three hundred people who've packed the bar and with a sweep of his hand invites me to join him. "Come on up here," Rome says. "Here he is, the winner of the First Annual Great American Smack-Off...JT the BRICK!"

Wearing my Mickey Mantle New York Yankees jersey, number 7 stenciled on the back, I raise my arms and plow through the crowd, riding the cheering, wild applause and chants of *"Brick," "JT," "Way to go!"* and *"Knicks suck!"* like a surfer on a wave. I arrive next to Rome and shake his hand. He steps aside and I address the crowd. "Thank you, Van Smack. All I can say, humbly, is that it's great to be the *King*!"

Insanity.

Moments later, I'm standing three deep at the bar, Jimmy B., Gerber, and a couple other of my boys at my side, mingling with *clones* who introduce themselves, congratulate me, and buy me shots, which we chase with beers and continuous orders of wings.

When we finish here, we'll move on to a second sports bar, and then a third, transported to each by a stretch limousine provided courtesy of *The Jim Rome Show*. When Joe Tutino called for my address a few days ago and explained that a limo would be picking me up and returning me to my apartment after the three events with Jim, a surprising jangle of nervousness overcame me. I felt the need for friendly faces around me.

"Would it be okay if I brought a few of my friends along?" I asked Tutino.

"Sure. Bring anybody you want."

And now, buoyed by my buddies, pushing through the mob that has jammed into the National Sports Grill, I stumble outside, half-drunk, and land in the center of the backseat of the stretch limousine.

"Do you believe this?" I say to the guys.

"You're like Mick fucking Jagger," one of them says.

"You know what, JT?" Jimmy says. "You can do this."

I think I understand what he means because I feel it, too, but I want him to clarify. "What? Do *what*?"

"This. You can do *this*. Sports talk."

"You mean, what? For a living?"

"Absolutely."

Either the back of the limo suddenly goes stony silent or I have drifted out of my body and I'm taking in what will be the most profound words I'd ever heard.

I sip my beer, wipe my mouth. "Maybe," I say, but what I mean and dare not say, at least not yet, is *Not only can I do this, I will.*

6.

Charlie Hustle

San Diego–Las Vegas
1995–1996

THREE HUNDRED COLD CALLS.

Twenty potential clients.

Ten qualified... qualified... qual—

I stare at my phone and I say quietly, "Qualified? For what? *I'm* no longer qualified." I slip off my headset, lay it on my desk, and stare at it. "I have to figure this out," I say.

And then, without a plan, without a script, on total instinct and putting my onions on the line, I snap the headset back on, find the number of the Mighty 690, and cold-call the program director.

He takes my call right away.

"JT the Brick, King of Smack," he says. "Great call. Everybody's talking about it."

"Thank you." I lean forward, lower my voice, and speak with

an urgency I've never felt before, ever, about anything. "See, the thing is, I want to do sports talk for a living. It kicked in for me when I won the Smack-Off. I got a passion for it. I can do this. I *know* I can do it. I just need a chance. If there was any way I could do something there, anything—"

"I don't have anything," he says, cutting me off. "And if I did, I'm not sure you're ready yet."

My world starts to cave in.

"But." He pauses. "I know a guy. Keith James. He runs a small FM station up in Pasadena, KMAX 1077. Sports talk. Mostly syndicated, but he goes local on the weekends and he might need somebody."

"Thank you, thank you very much, I'm gonna call him. *Thank you.*"

I click off and feel the guy in the next cubicle looking at me.

"I don't know how you do it, JT," he says. "I'm batting like oh for two hundred today."

"Never stop calling," I say. "Your next call might be the one."

———

"I have my own radio show."

The next Saturday afternoon, alone in my car, driving the freeway from Pasadena, a suburb of Los Angeles, to La Jolla, a three-hour drive if there's no traffic, I say those words aloud. And then I shout them.

"I have my own radio show!"

Okay, I admit, it's not much of a radio show.

I will be on the air once a week for two hours, every Sunday night, ten to midnight, not exactly prime time, but still—

I HAVE MY OWN RADIO SHOW!

Did I mention that I'll be doing my own radio show for free?

Technically, that's not true. When I add up how much it will cost in gas to drive to Pasadena and back every Sunday night, I'll actually be in the hole.

Is this how Howard Stern started? Or Mike and the Mad Dog? Or Jim Rome?

It doesn't matter.

Because this is how I'm starting.

And I know right out of the gate that I'm *killing*. I've found my passion. I can't wait for Sunday night.

Six weeks in, my boss leaves me a voice message, says he needs to meet with me. On my drive in I obsess over what he wants to tell me. I figure it can't be bad. If he were firing me, he'd do it in a phone call. And I'm certain he's not firing me. I know I'm still raw on the radio, but I blast through those two hours with drive and energy, taking call after call from a steady flow of flashing phone lines and offering up sizzling-hot opinions and sports takes as overheated as my winning Smack-Off call. No. He's not firing me. Just the opposite. In fact, I know what he's going to do. He's going to start paying me.

"You're gonna have to start paying me," he says.

I sit across from my boss and go limp, immobile, and momentarily mute. I finally manage to speak. "I have to *pay* you?"

"Yeah. Look, you're doing great. I love your show. But I can't give you this time slot for free anymore. I gotta start charging you."

"I'm trying to get my head around this. I'm doing good, so as a reward I have to give you money."

"That's it. Now you got it."

"No offense, but this is fucked up."

My boss shrugs, starts patting his shirt pocket as if he's looking for a pack of cigarettes. "Welcome to radio."

"How much?"

"Two hundred bucks an hour."

"So, four hundred bucks a week?"

"Take it or leave it."

An idea wriggles its way into my muddled mind.

"Can I have sponsors? Can I do commercials?"

My boss does something with his face that may or may not be a frown. "I don't care what you do. I just need a check for four hundred bucks every Sunday night. Leave it inside the safe. And make sure you don't miss a week."

"I won't. Thanks. I guess."

"Don't mention it. And, hey, I think you got a bright future."

———

Monday morning, I slam the Los Angeles yellow pages down on my desk, flip through the ads, and rack my brain. Within seconds, inspiration hits. I riffle to the front of the alphabet until I arrive at companies that sell bricks. I cold-call a couple who've never heard of me, the Smack-Off, or Jim Rome, and they tell me to get lost. Third time's a charm. I call a company named Higgins Bricks. The son of Mr. Higgins himself answers the phone. As I begin my spiel, he interrupts me. He not only knows who I am, he happens to be a *clone*.

"Awesome call, Brick," he says, echoing Jim Rome. "Epic scud."

"Appreciate it," I say, and then I launch into my pitch, explaining how I've just landed my own show and that I'm looking for sponsors.

"Totally epic. How much for a spot?"

"Four hundred bucks," I say, and hold my breath.

"That all? No problem."

I pump my fist. I thank him, hang up, and even though I've hit my quota with one call, I cold-call a few other companies, including a car wash and a dry cleaner. I get a couple more to commit. I add up my sponsors and come up with $700, enough to cover the $400 to pay for my airtime, plus gas and dinner.

I'm starting to get the hang of this radio business.

In August, three months after I've begun moonlighting from Merrill as a sports talk host, Keith James, my KMAX boss, calls me again.

"Got something for you," he says. "My midday guys are going on vacation next week. If you wanna come up, you could fill in for them, noon to three, all week. A one-shot deal."

"Wow. Really?"

"Really. Yes or no."

"Depends. How much is this gonna cost me?"

I think he stifles a laugh. Hard to tell over the phone. "Nothing," he says. "Actually, I'll pay you a little money, make it worth your while."

"*You're* gonna pay *me?*"

"Don't get used to it."

"Don't worry. I wouldn't want to get spoiled."

I hang up, head into my boss's office at Merrill, and arrange to take a week of vacation. Then I contact my friend Andy who lives in Long Beach and tell him I'm in a jam and I need a favor. He invites me to crash at his place for the week, cutting down my daily commute from three hours to an hour and a half, saving my life.

One minute into my first day on the noon-to-three shift, I'm baffled. I enter the radio station, scan the area, and stop dead. It appears that during the day the radio station hums with *people*—real live actual humans—sitting at desks, working, writing, speaking on the phone and to one another, offering me something to drink, showing me the studio, laughing at something I say. In contrast to the silence I'm accustomed to at night, I'm bombarded now by noise, the sounds of computers clacking, fax machines humming, telephones jangling, a boss shouting, and then a rush of smells: coffee, maple-syrupy doughnuts, cigarette smoke, and liberal doses of perfume, air freshener, and sweat. I have never associated radio with such *life*. Until now radio has meant solitude, my voice echoing back to me in the cold and dark, a life existing alone—by choice—like some willing castaway. Being an extremely social being, creating and becoming defined by a brotherhood, and taking pride in my tight circle of friends, I felt that accepting the solitude of radio was the one compromise I would have to make. But now I see that radio doesn't have to be that way. It can be a social environment, a community. At least it feels that way now, during daylight. And so I am baffled. And then, a blink later, I am thrilled.

I enter the studio and meet my engineer and my producer and we work out today's show. The producer starts to line up a few guests and we discuss music cues, play-ins, play-outs, and for the first time I feel as if I'm doing an actual *show*. Once we start, the lines light up, the listeners call in, and I'm off and running. I have no need to imagine lonely insomniacs listening to me at home or driving dark empty highways to or from their jobs on the graveyard shift. I can see my audience right outside my door. Any slight doubt I may have had about making radio my career evaporates. I caught the radio bug before. After this week, I'm infected by it.

On Friday, after my last show, my boss thanks me for stepping in and for stepping up and hands me an envelope.

"What's this?" I say.

"Around here we call it a paycheck. Remember, don't get used to it."

"I won't," I say, but I'm lying.

I'm going to get used to it. I vow to work in radio full-time, and I will get paid.

———

I return to Merrill and to La Jolla and resume driving three hours to Pasadena every Sunday night for my once-a-week gig. A couple of Sundays after my weeklong paid substitute job, I notice something odd one afternoon when I balance my checkbook.

My bank hasn't cleared the last check I placed in the safe at the radio station.

I double-check my bank statement and confirm. Yes. The bank has skipped that check number.

The next Sunday night before my show, I open the safe and prepare to slide in my check and...I stop.

In the safe I see my last check.

My boss hasn't opened the safe in a week.

And then it happens.

I sense *trouble* like a familiar toxic smell blowing in.

I allow the sense of trouble to settle and then I place this week's check on top of last week's. If this one doesn't clear, I know I'm close to making a move.

A week later both checks lie in the safe untouched.

On the drive home, I come up with a theory.

My boss has stopped cashing my checks because the station's in trouble. A good guy at heart, he's doing me a favor and sending me a message.

JT, your four hundred bucks a week can't save this sinking ship. The money's better off in your pocket than in mine.

Translation: the station is going down.

The following Sunday I finish the show trying to tamp down my slowly growing low-level-grade anxiety. The next morning I call the producer I worked with during my week filling in at the station and ask if he's heard any office gossip about the station being in trouble. He lowers his voice and mumbles that rumors are flying. Most likely scenario: The owners have put the station up for sale and buyers are circling. Everyone's on edge.

I allow myself one second of self-pity, floating the "I'm just getting started and the station falls apart" whine through my brain, and then brush that off and jump into action. I know I can't find work at the Mighty 690—according to their program director I'm not *ready*—so I call the other sports talk station in San Diego, KFMB, home of the San Diego Padres. I ask for the program director, Dave Sniff. He gets right on the line. He knows my story and knows I've been working at KMAX. I tell him the station's on the brink of being sold and I'm looking for a steady gig, something closer to home. I'm starting to wear down from stockbroking all week and driving back and forth to Pasadena every Sunday night. He tells me to send him a tape. I put together a compilation package of highlights from my shows and my Smack-Off call, pop the tape into priority mail, wait two days, and call him again.

"Heard the tape," Dave says. "Come in this afternoon."

Sitting with Dave in his office, I allow myself a brief fantasy, which I quickly bat away. In my reverie, he offers me a full-time job that actually pays a living wage, allowing me to quit Merrill.

"I have something for you," Dave says. "It's not ideal. Sunday night, seven to ten."

"Are you kidding? It's perfect. I'll take it."

"Great." Dave shifts in his chair. "Now the awkward part. The money."

I shift in my chair. Together our butts make the seats sing an off-key vinyl duet.

"I'm gonna have to charge you five hundred bucks."

I'm not sure if the whooshing sound that follows comes from me or the chair.

"Wow. Five hundred bucks."

Unbelievable. Every time I land a job in radio it costs me *more*. I'm not sure how much longer I can afford this career.

I somehow manage to smile. "As long as I can get sponsors, I got no problem with the five hundred."

"Great. You start next week. Let's check out your studio."

I follow Dave to a small studio around the corner. A guy with a Ted Baxter shock of white hair fiddles with some controls. He stands when we come in. He's tall, fit, and looks like he's played some football.

"Hey, Ted," Dave says. "Meet JT. He's taking over the Sunday night shift."

"Excellent," the man says, and puts out his hand. "Ted Leitner."

I reach over and shake his hand, trying to maintain some cool. Ted Leitner is the voice of the Padres, a local legend. He pauses as a flicker of recognition forms in his eyes. "JT the *Brick*?"

"Yeah," I say. "Pleasure meeting you. You're amazing. I love listening to you."

"Well, I've been at it awhile. But, hey, I wish I had half your energy."

"Thanks, I'm still trying to figure the rest out," I say.

"You will. Just keep at it."

"Appreciate it," I say. Ted, the consummate pro and someone I truly respect, hasn't said that much, but in this simple exchange he's validated me enough to shoot me out of the building and into the parking lot feeling high.

That night I meet Jimmy Baxter for a celebratory beer and to figure out my financial life, which currently lies in shambles.

"You gotta pay five hundred for this job?" he says. "You only paid four for the last one."

"It's a way better station," I say.

"Got it. The better the station, the more you pay. Try not to work at a really excellent station, though, or you'll go broke."

I roll my eyes, raise a finger for another beer. "Yeah, well, that's the real problem. Seriously. In two months, Merrill stops paying me. My thirty-grand incentive they gave me? Gone. In order to live, I'm either gonna have to break into my IRA or—"

"Ask your dad for a loan."

We sip our beers quietly. We know we've hit a dead end. Of course, I could ask my dad for a loan...and I can't. I just can't. At some point soon, I will have to explain to him that I have given up on becoming a stockbroker because I've discovered my passion, a career that feeds my soul. Sports talk radio.

Right.

I might as well tell him I'm jumping aboard the space shuttle and relocating to the moon so I can prospect for moondust, that's how foreign and insane a career in sports talk radio will seem to him.

"If I weren't fucking *paying* to work, I might be able to explain it to him." My taste for celebration turns sour. I suddenly feel small and impotent.

"It will happen," Jimmy says.

I look at him.

"It has to," he says, looking me straight in the eye. "Only a matter of time. You're too good."

I nod, not because he's right but because he's my best friend and I need him and he's *there*. Whether he means what he said or not, he's blowing just the right amount of smoke up my ass. That's what best friends do.

"Thanks," I say. "That means a lot."

"You bought that shit?"

I crack up. We order another round. We change the subject, talk sex and sports.

And somehow I know it's gonna be all right.

⟶

In my cubicle at Merrill, I whip open the San Diego yellow pages and strap on my headset. Because they're located close to Los Angeles, Higgins Bricks and my other sponsors have bailed, so I need to find a new roster of sponsors for my Sunday night show on KFMB. This day I'm on fire and I line up a good mix of the usual suspects, a dry cleaner, a car wash, a pizza joint, an auto supply store, totaling a neat $800, covering my expenses and then some. Then, guilt gnaws at me because I'm working on my show on company time and I make another three hundred cold calls all for Merrill, even though my heart's not in it and I'm running on fumes. I leave work after the stock market closes feeling both drained and wired. I have a week to prepare for my first show on KFMB. I promise myself that I will be more than ready. I vow to blow them away.

Each afternoon after my morning at Merrill Lynch, I work on my show. The first day, I sit down with a legal pad and break my three hours into segments, fifteen minutes each, four each hour, twelve segments in all. Looking at the chart I've drawn, I feel overwhelmed. *Twelve* segments? What the hell am I gonna talk about in all of those segments? How will I move the show along, keep my energy up? I decide to focus on one segment at a time. So, first segment. What to do? What do the pros do? I remember turning on the car radio after work and hearing a sports talk radio team's first segment. I replay it in my head.

"Welcome to the show," the first guy said, call him Fred. "So, how was your weekend, Bob?"

"Not bad, Fred. Stayed home, watched TV with the wife. Soccer with the kids. You?"

"Pretty much the same. Got a massage. My back went out."

"Oh, yeah, a little rub-a-dub-dub for your *back*. Right. HA!"

"I'm not going there, Bob. No way. The wife might be listening."

"Ha-HA! Gotcha. So, hey, Fred, how about the traffic on the five freeway coming in, huh?"

"The worst. I got stuck in it, too."

"A parking lot. Brutal."

This is sports talk?

No.

Just no.

I refuse to do any version of this.

I will talk sports, serious sports, and sports only.

Then I think about Hacksaw and his opening monologue and I'm inspired. For the first fifteen minutes he lets loose a nonstop torrent of sports news. The amount of information he feeds you is staggering. I decide to start each hour with a monologue of my own, but more opinion than fact, recapping the week's most important sports stories laced with my own hot Smack-Off stream of consciousness. I have no producer—I'll be alone in the studio—and I can't count on booking guests myself, especially on Sunday night, so I will devote my remaining nine segments to callers. I study my legal pad and consider the show in these smaller fifteen-minute blocks, and the three hours seem much more manageable. The next day I go to Staples on my way home from work and buy several sheets of oak tag and a glue stick. Then I stop at the newsstand near my apartment and load up on weekly sports magazines and all the newspapers.

I cut out articles and headlines and glue them onto a piece of oak tag. I arrange the important stories in the center of the poster and fan out from there, sticking the less pressing stories and less popular sports in the corners. Hockey, for example, finds its home in the upper left. By the end of the week, I've completely covered this sheet of white oak tag with sports stories, creating an oversize action-packed cue card.

My first Sunday night, I drive the short distance to the radio station, arriving fifteen minutes before my seven o'clock shift. I park as close as I can to the door of the building, drag out my piece of oak tag, tuck the poster under my arm, and enter the studio. Inside, I place the poster right in front of me for easy reference. The show starts and I launch into my monologue. I flit from story to story on my poster, but after I finish the monologue and get into the flow of the show, I rely less on the poster and more on the callers.

The three hours zoom by. At ten I sign off, more charged up than when I started at seven. I pull off my headset just as the engineer's muffled monotone mutters, "Good show." I start to say thanks, but I know he's already out of the building and halfway to his car. I pack up my poster, tuck it under my arm, and walk toward my car, beaming a halogen smile that nothing can dim. I veer to the side of the building and stop at the station's Dumpster. I rip the oak tag into pieces and flip them into the garbage. And so my first show on a major radio station ends. On to the next, more determined than ever that tonight is truly the beginning.

Five weeks and five oak tag posters later, I sit in my apartment facing a fiscal cliff.

I have entered my last month at Merrill. After that, I will have no more money coming in. I want my radio gig to work, and except for the nearly comical twist that I have to pay five hundred dollars a week to keep the gig, I think it is working. Separately, Dave Sniff, my boss, and Ted Leitner have told me that they like what they hear and to keep doing what I'm doing. Unfortunately, I'm a month away from telling them I can no longer afford my infant radio career.

There has to be a way I can make this work, I think.

And then, sitting in my apartment, I come up with an idea. I will do what I do best.

Cold-call.

I will cold-call the Sports Fan Radio Network.

I'll call the Las Vegas company that syndicates sports talk, such as their flagship show, *The Pete Rose Show*, over a bundle of stations across the country, among them KMAX, the place I bolted from in Pasadena.

In a frenzy, I dial information in Las Vegas and get the number for Sports Fan Radio. I call immediately and ask the switchboard operator for the network's program director.

"Charlie Barker," she tells me. "I'll connect you."

I clear my throat, stand, and pace.

It hits me then like a slap.

I'm about to make the most important cold call of my life.

"Charlie Barker," his secretary says.

I hang up.

I'm not ready.

I have to prepare for this call the way I prepped for the Smack-Off. I know I can get past the secretary and get Charlie Barker on the phone—I do that three hundred times a day—but I will have one chance to sell Charlie Barker. I can't blow it.

Because I know that if I don't score with this call—if I don't turn this cold call into a qualified lead—I will have to leave California and go back home.

The image of that—picturing myself packing up my apartment, saying good-bye to Jimmy and Bobby G. and the Home Wrecker and moving back home to start over, doing I have no idea what, ignites me. I grab a legal pad and start scribbling notes, creating my script. Finished, satisfied, I take a deep breath, dial Sports Fan Radio, and ask for Charlie Barker's extension. I sweet-talk my way past his secretary and within seconds he comes on the line.

"This is Charlie Barker."

"Mr. Barker, my name is John Tournour. You may know me as JT the Brick on KFMB in San Diego—"

And I'm off.

I'm roaring, a force of nature. In my mind I grab Charlie by the shirt and refuse to let him go. I tell him that I need to take the next step in my career because I'm about to take off—I'm about to *explode*—and I want to be a part of the Sports Fan Radio Network.

I pause to catch my breath. I've hit him with all I've got. I wait for him to make the next move.

Silence.

Come on, Charlie, I think. *Say something. Say ANYTHING. Come ON.*

Finally, Charlie speaks. "Well," he says, "I certainly hear your passion." He pauses again—forever—then says, "Okay. Send me a tape."

Now I pause.

"I'd rather not do that," I say.

"No?"

"I'd rather see you in person. I'd like to meet you and give you the tape myself. I'll fly to Vegas—"

"Actually, I'll be in Los Angeles in two weeks doing a remote with Pete Rose at Planet Hollywood."

"Perfect," I say. "I'll come up and meet you and hand you the tape."

"Great," Charlie says.

"Outstanding," I say. "I look forward to meeting you, and thank you very much for—"

I stop because I realize I'm talking to a dial tone.

Two weeks later, wearing a suit and with a new haircut, I burst out of the office and drive three hours north to Hollywood. I swing into the parking lot at Planet Hollywood, reluctantly hand the keys of my Porsche to the shady-looking valet, and enter the restaurant in search of Charlie Barker.

I see Pete Rose first. Headset clamped over his familiar round face, his body still thick as a fullback's, the player known as Charlie Hustle sits camped behind a table on the stage talking baseball into a microphone. He breaks for a commercial and fans swarm the stage, ten, twenty of them, offering up sheets of papers, baseballs, and items of clothing, which he graciously signs.

I walk to the stage and stop a long-haired guy wearing a plastic press pass on a cloth lanyard around his neck.

"Excuse me. I'm here to see Charlie Barker."

The guy grunts and tilts his head toward the engineer, a surprisingly young-looking man wearing a headset and sitting at the far end of Pete Rose's table. I hop onto the stage and approach Charlie. He sees me coming and lowers his headset to his shoulders.

"Charlie?" I say. "JT. We spoke on the phone."

Charlie smiles and we shake hands. "Can't believe you drove up here," he says. "Hey, hold on. Pete! Say hello to JT the Brick."

I cross the stage to Pete Rose in two steps. I reach out my hand and Major League Baseball's all-time hit leader grips it, pumps it, and flashes me a wide smile. "Nice to see you."

He pulls away and returns to signing autographs and kibitzing with fans. I head back to Charlie Barker. "I brought you my tape," I say. "Also brought the Smack-Off call and my résumé."

"Thanks. I promise to check it all out." Charlie glances at his watch and starts to slide the headset up his neck. "We're back on. I'll get back to you."

"When?"

Charlie freezes. He smiles, but I can tell by his eyes that this smile is a cover. He's either impressed by how forward I am or soured by it. "It's gonna take me probably a week or two—"

"I don't have that kind of time," I say. "My clock's ticking. Any way I can follow up with you a little sooner?"

"Give me a week," Charlie says. He clamps on his headset and turns away.

I call him the next day.

"I just wanted to thank you for taking the time to meet with me," I say. "I know you probably haven't heard the tape yet, but I want to tell you how much I appreciate your doing this."

"Not a problem," Charlie says, but this time I sense a trace of warmth in his voice. "I'll get back to you soon. Within a week. I promise."

I thank him and hang up.

Charlie calls me back one week to the day. "I heard the tape," he says. "I got something for you."

⎯⎯⎯

He flies me to Las Vegas the following weekend and puts me up at the MGM Grand, where Sports Fan Radio Network broadcasts nationally from the casino's sports book. Charlie has given me my shot, a two-show audition for the overnight weekend shift, Friday and Saturday, midnight to five a.m. If he hires me,

Charlie will not only fly me to and from Vegas, he will also *pay* me. All I have to do is kill on the radio.

I kill.

He doesn't even have to hear the second show.

He offers me the job after the first show.

The Monday I return, I break the news to Dave Sniff, my boss at KFMB, who says, "You're on your way. Happy I got you started."

"I'll never forget that," I say.

That night I call my dad. I tell him I have found my passion and I'm doing everything I can to turn my passion into a full-time paid position.

"Go for it," he says.

He doesn't say he has my back. He doesn't have to.

———

Friday night. Eleven thirty. I power through a casino the size of a football field on the way to my first show of my first weekend in Las Vegas. I weave in and out of the people packed around the gaming tables, the players and tourists and stragglers and cocktail waitresses and dealers trading shifts. I stop at the rim of the sports book, look back, and allow the sounds and smells of the night to envelop me—the whir and chime and clanging of the slot machines, a cheer rising up around a crowded craps table, the perfume of a squadron of cocktail waitresses slashing through the low-hanging cloud of cigarette smoke. I take it all in and my body hums with excitement.

I make my way through the sports book to the makeshift

studio, introduce myself to my producer, and settle in for my five-hour shift. For the first time in months, I have not written out my show on a sheet of oak tag. Instead I spent four hours in my hotel room before the show scribbling notes on a legal pad, jotting bullet points for my monologue, circling topics for each hour and for each segment.

The late night guy leaves. I wriggle on my headset and on the producer's cue burn into my monologue, my volume taking off like a rocket, blasting away everyone in the immediate area. I settle in, and as the time passes I become dimly aware of a hunger rising in me, a hunger that begins to grow every hour, becoming by show's end a persistent gnawing at my insides.

It's not enough, I realize. *It doesn't feed me. I need more.*

The weekend shift is not enough.

I hunger for more.

⸺

I don't start hounding Charlie right away.

I wait a month.

I know I can't hit him too hard at first. I have to ease in, float what I want casually, allow the idea to simmer, and then turn up the heat.

What do I want?

The weekday gig.

That's not technically true. The truth is—

The weekday gig *belongs* to me.

I see the guy who has it now as a placeholder. He's merely keeping the seat warm until Charlie sees that he has to remove him and move me over from weekends. Charlie just doesn't know it yet.

I call Charlie from Merrill during the week. We talk about the show. He tells me that he loves what I'm doing. He couldn't be happier. I thank him and say, casually, "I've been on for a month now and I feel I'm ready for something full-time."

"I'll keep that in mind," Charlie says.

I hammer Charlie as subtly as I can, but I do hammer him. It never occurs to me that I might be coming on too strong. I know only that I have to be on the radio every night, five nights a week. No. I *deserve* to be on five nights a week. I know that Charlie knows it, too. And so I pitch him. I sell him as if he's a potential client and I'm trying to move him off the dime, turn him into a qualified lead. I'm pushing a stock that I insist he buy before it shoots up too high in price and he misses out. Except this time I'm not selling a stock. I'm selling myself.

Six weeks in, the money Merrill fronted me long gone, Charlie calls me. "I don't know why, but I get the feeling you wouldn't mind working overnights during the week."

"Where'd you get that idea?"

"Call it a hunch." He holds for a second. "I got the approval. We're gonna make you an offer. Our business guy will call you tomorrow."

I want to leap up in my cubicle, sprint, and scream, but somehow I keep my excitement in check.

"Thank you for the opportunity, Charlie," I say.

The business guy calls the next day and makes it official. Sports Fan Radio offers me a full-time gig, Monday to Friday, midnight to five a.m.

For this they will pay me $25,000 a year.

"Wow," I say. "That's gonna be tough. I'm not sure I can survive on that. Here at Merrill I can make six figures if I hustle, easily. I'd be walking away from that. Twenty-five grand a year, huh? Plus I gotta move to Vegas."

"We can help with that," the business guy says.

"Okay, that's good, thank you. This is a great opportunity, don't get me wrong. I'm just a little concerned about the finances."

"That's all I got," the business guy says. "That's all we have in the budget for that time slot."

"I appreciate the offer. I have to think about it. Can I call you tomorrow?"

"Absolutely. No problem. Take a day to think about it."

I hang up and call my dad. In a rush of nervousness and excitement I spew out the details—that I've received a legitimate offer for a full-time job doing sports talk, that I will have to move to Vegas, and that the company will pay me $25,000 a year.

He hesitates. "Can you push them to thirty?" he says.

"I don't think so. I don't have a lot of leverage. I don't want to lose the job over five grand."

"You need to ask for a little more," my dad says. "You have to act like you're worth more than that. And you are."

"So, I have your support?"

"Of course," he says. "It's your dream."

The next morning I call the business guy back. "I want to do this," I say. "But I need to get at least thirty thousand."

"I can't do that," he says. "I can go to twenty-seven five. We'll also pay for your move and your first month's rent. How's that?"

"Done deal," I say.

I hang up, feeling more energized than I have in years. "Here we go," I say to myself. "It's time to go. Time to get to work."

My head spinning, I stand up in my cubicle and survey the bull pen on either side of me. I allow one unexpected moment of nostalgia to seep in and pass, and then a fistful of fear suddenly clutches my heart.

There's no way the Merrill brass will let me walk without paying back the up-front money they gave me. They're going to want the $30,000 back.

I don't have it. I will have to sell my car, or ask my dad, or . . . I don't know what . . . but I can't ask my dad. He may have the money to lend me but I don't have the heart to ask him for it.

And then I find myself walking down the corridor on the side of the bull pen, arriving outside the door of the large corner office belonging to Bob, the guy above Jerry, the big boss, the man who runs the La Jolla branch of Merrill. Bob, like most people in the office, has been following my sports talk radio addiction with curiosity. He appreciates my work ethic and my consistent play at third base on the softball team.

I poke my head inside his office. "Hey, Bob, do you have a second?"

Sitting at his desk, absorbed in paperwork, he looks up and waves me in.

I shut the door behind me.

"I have some exciting news and I wanted to tell you first—"

"Sit down, JT."

I lower myself into the chair facing his desk. Sweat begins to leak into my palms. I rub my hands on my pants.

Bob kicks back in his chair. "What's on your mind?"

"You know I've been fascinated with sports talk radio ever since I won that caller contest. I've actually been picking up some work on the side. Well, I just got an offer to move to Las Vegas to work full-time. I'm going to be syndicated nationwide by a company called Sports Fan Radio Network."

Bob smiles, a genuinely warm, affectionate smile. "You taking it?"

"I have to. It's the opportunity of a lifetime. I can't turn it down."

"You sure? You could really make it as a broker if you wanted to."

"That's just it. I don't. My heart's not in it. I want to do radio."

"Then all I can do is wish you luck." Bob stands and comes around from behind his desk. I stand up to meet him. He reaches out his hand and we shake warmly. "It's been a pleasure knowing you, JT," he says. "Stay in touch."

"I will. Thanks."

"There is one other thing. The thirty thousand we gave you."

My heart starts pumping and the sweat returns to my palms. "I know. I—"

"Forget it. Consider that a signing bonus."

"Wow. Thank you. I'm speechless."

Bob grins, bangs me on the back. "Don't let that happen on the radio."

That same afternoon, over pitchers of beer at Lahaina Beach House, we celebrate, the guys of DK West, Jimmy, Bobby G., the Home Wrecker, and all the rest of the crew. We toast to my upcoming new life and my relocation. We get loud and raucous, and as if we are part of the Rat Pack, Bobby G. raises his glass and calls out, "We're expanding, boys. Taking new territory. We got a guy in Vegas now." Later, with music blasting out of the shell of the restaurant, the blazing orange sun falling into the sea, I find myself standing on the beach next to Jimmy, the way we stood on a similar beach seven years earlier.

"I'm happy for you," Jimmy says. "You found what you're looking for."

"Thanks. What about you?"

"Still looking."

"Well, you know, you have to come to Vegas often—"

"A given," Jimmy says.

"Good."

"You're on a roll, JT," Jimmy says. "Keep it going."

Shoulder to shoulder, we watch the sun die, turning the horizon deep purple and then black. We say nothing for a long time. Finally, without a word, the two of us, best friends, inseparable since elementary school, walk back into the bar and join the rest of the crew, knowing that, in a few days when I hit the road for Vegas, we will be apart for the first time in our lives.

7.

Gorilla on Line One

Las Vegas
1996

RIGHT BEFORE I leave La Jolla for Las Vegas, my Porsche's engine blows up. Once again, the DKs save me. Hercy, a former fraternity brother, a car guy, somehow rebuilds the engine so I can turn the car in to Porsche leasing without going into bankruptcy. He also finds me a cheap, reliable used car, which I buy, a piece of shit that quacks when it finds fourth gear. I pack the Daffymobile with all my belongings, not even enough stuff to fill a suitcase, and haul ass to Vegas.

Dave, a friend of a friend, rents me a room in his apartment, a short walk from the studio at the MGM Grand, where I work from midnight until five a.m., Monday through Friday. I buy a crappy mattress—no box spring, no bed frame, no headboard—one towel, a few toiletries. I can't afford dishes, silverware, a pot, or a pan. I eat my meals at the $1.99 all-

98

you-can-eat buffet across the street at Ellis Island, a small off-the-Strip motel and casino.

On weekends and before I begin my show at midnight, I frequent the center bar at the Hard Rock Cafe, the hottest spot on the Strip, where bands like Mötley Crüe hang out. I hang with Todd, the head bartender, a transplant from upstate New York and fellow Knicks fanatic, a caller to my show, who becomes a close friend and running mate. We meet after he calls the show one night and on the air invites me to drop in for a drink. I sign off, walk over to the Hard Rock, and make my way to the center bar, where Todd pours drinks and shoots the shit with Nikki Sixx, Tommy Lee, and Vince Neil. I introduce myself to Todd. He shoots out from behind the bar, pumps my hand, introduces me to the band, and comps my drinks. In a matter of weeks, Todd brings me into his circle of high-rolling bartenders and off-the-hook partiers.

"We got the bars covered in this town," he says, clapping me on the back one night, pouring me yet another complimentary cocktail. "We need a guy like you in our crew."

He and his guys remind me of Bobby G. and our own ragtag Rat Pack, which I consider the ultimate compliment. As if to prove this point, I gather with Todd and his Wild Bunch, my new crew now, in the kitchen of the Hard Rock Cafe one slow midafternoon. In suits, we pose for a photograph, re-creating a movie still from the original *Ocean's 11*, which starred Frank Sinatra, Sammy Davis, Dean Martin, and the rest of *the* Rat Pack.

As much as I live to party with Todd and his crew—guys who welcome Jimmy, Bobby G., the Home Wrecker, and any of my other friends into their circle whenever they visit—I approach my work with laser focus and enough energy to power a train. Beginning with my monologue, I whip through each hour, somehow gaining strength as the night goes on, ending the show with a segment I call Speed Brick, a series of rapid ten-second rants from overheated callers. I go home or to the Hard Rock spent, wrung out, having left every ounce of me at the studio. I crash at dawn or just after, careful not to get too blotto during the workweek, grab a solid four or five hours—all I need—wake, blink away the morning after, shower, shave, grab a coffee and a paper across the street, and jot down notes for the upcoming night's show.

I also spend time studying my list of affiliate stations in the network. I want to plug in to them somehow. I want them to know me. I start to think about the next step in my career, how to make more money and maybe move out of overnights and into working during the day. Overall, I'm a jangling nerve ending, hyped up, restless.

I'm able at least to plot my radio future, if not realize it, because I find a kindred spirit in my board operator, Bobby Machado, a long-haired, wiry, tatted-up ball of fire from Boston whose fingers fly over the controls and buttons like a mad keyboardist. Bobby, a cross between Steve Buscemi and Steven Tyler, wears hoodies and Red Sox caps and sunglasses, even at night, and whenever he walks into a room I catch a whiff of cigarette smoke. Walking home early one morning after a hot show run by Bobby and a breakfast of blueberry pancakes with—and paid for by—Todd, I say aloud to the sun beginning to appear over the mountains at the end of the desert, "You found Todd, you got Bobby, you got lucky."

A few months in, heading into the heart of the show, I hit a topic that heats up the phone lines. Segments fly by while Bobby screens each call and I spar with each caller. In the middle of a segment, I notice Bobby nodding into his phone for what seems like a long time, and then he puts the call on hold. I go to commercial and Bobby, who's sitting across from me in the cramped studio, says, "There's a guy on hold who claims to be the program director from WQAM in Miami."

"WQAM? That's a big affiliate."

"Major."

I fiddle with my headset cord. "What's he want?"

Bobby pulls off his Red Sox cap and gathers up a handful of split ends. "Didn't say."

"Charlie doesn't want me talking to program directors," I say. "He says it's bad form. He got pissed when I called Bob Agnew in San Francisco. Plus, what the fuck time is it? This program director is up, listening to *me*?"

Bobby tugs his cap back on and yanks down the brim. "Want me to get rid of him?"

"Fuck it. I'll talk to him."

I glance at the clock. Less than a minute to air. I place the phone against my ear and press down line one. "Hey, this is JT."

"Yeah, babe."

For some reason, those two words knock my guard down.

"Andrew Ashwood, program director at WQAM in Miami. How you doing?"

"Great. Doing great. How you doing?"

"Good, babe, good. Hey, I'm listening to your show. I like what I hear."

"Thank you. Appreciate that."

I look at the clock again. I want to confirm the time.

One thirteen a.m.

Four thirteen a.m. in Miami.

"You got something. Seriously. I listen to a lot of radio at night, and obviously you're on my station, so I'm aware of you. I like to keep tabs on what's going on."

I try to conjure up a picture of this guy and draw a blank. Most program directors I've met are clean-cut, buttoned-up, nine-to-five guys in suits. I can't imagine that they routinely get up at four in the morning to listen to their overnight guy. Clearly, Andrew Ashwood is no nine-to-fiver, and I get the feeling that he's far from buttoned up.

"Hey, babe, I know you gotta get back on the air, but I wanna get your home address. I'd like to send you out something in the mail."

"And what would that be?"

"My playbook."

I hold a beat. "Okay, I'm not sure I—"

"It's my view of radio and where we are today in sports. Pointers. Dos and don'ts. Things I've picked up over the years. You might find it interesting."

"Well, yeah," I say. "It does sound...interesting."

"After you read it, give me a call. We'll talk about it."

Bobby lowers his sunglasses, waggles a finger in front of me, and nods at the clock. Fifteen seconds until air. I give Andrew Ashwood my address and throw in my phone number. He thanks me and hangs up.

"Seems like a nice guy," I say to Bobby, and then I'm back on the air and Andrew Ashwood falls off my radar.

A week later the doorbell rings and a bulging manila envelope lands with a thud outside the apartment door.

I tear open the package and find a thick spiral-bound notebook stuffed with articles snipped out of newspapers covering every aspect of radio. Andrew's playbook. He has divided his playbook into chapters made up of subjects such as how to be a radio host, the best ways to do a radio show, how radio works, demographics, and how radio has evolved in the 1990s.

I read the entire playbook from cover to cover.

I keep it on the floor next to my pillow.

After I read it, I go through it again, jotting notes, comparing my notes to notes Andrew's scribbled in the margins of articles and passages he's underlined. Andrew's playbook becomes my go-to reference, my radio bible.

A week after I receive the playbook—two weeks after he calls me in the studio—I call Andrew from my apartment. "Hey, Andrew. It's JT."

"Yeah, babe, how you doing? Did you dig the playbook?"

"It's tremendous. Amazing the time you spent, the amount of work you put into it."

"Yeah, well, thanks. It's a bunch of stuff I compiled over the years. Obviously, you don't have to read it cover to cover. You can cherry-pick here and there."

"I did," I say.

"Oh, okay, good."

"I did read it cover to cover."

"Huh." He pauses. "Then, okay, if there's anything you want to talk about, if you have any questions—"

"I got a lot of questions."

I hear him shift in his chair, a squeak of leather whooshing through the phone, and then I hear him sip a coffee or some other beverage. I can almost feel him relax. "Shoot."

I ask him questions about the business, about the biggest players on air and off, about who's hot and who's not. I ask him about programming strategies, scheduling, salaries. Andrew bats back every question with a fast and furious and well-thought-out answer. He offers advice and warns me of certain pitfalls. He owns a wealth of information and spews it like a geyser. He withholds nothing. He says that I'm talented but raw and he can see that I'm also driven. He tells me that my energy is my ace, but I have to learn to modulate both that and my volume. He lowers his voice to make the point that sometimes a whisper works better than a scream. He explains that it's crucial for me to maintain a clear vision and create a career path and insists that I never waver from either. He is patient and passionate and I am a sponge.

We talk for more than an hour.

"I have to go into a meeting," Andrew says finally. "No bullshit. I'm not blowing you off. I really do have a meeting."

"Oh, okay, well, thank you. I really appreciate your time."

"Call me anytime. Call me tomorrow."

I do.

We talk for another hour.

We continue speaking about the business, but this time we also talk sports. He's as insane for the Green Bay Packers as I am for the Yankees and Knicks. We talk as student and mentor and as colleagues, but we also talk as friends. We promise to talk again in a few days.

We hang up and I think, *Where would I be without the freaking phone?* And then I say aloud, "Damn. How about that? Andrew cold-called *me*."

And so it begins.

———

According to Andrew, the Sports Fan Radio Network tilts heavily in the direction of Pete Rose. They have anointed him their anchor, their cleanup hitter, their major investment. In our rudimentary math, the network is paying Pete a salary that works out to more than all the other hosts' salaries *combined*. This seems way out of whack when we consider that Pete's entire contribution amounts to a two-hour radio show, four days a week. Bottom line: the company has put all their chips on Charlie Hustle.

My move is clear.

Figure out how to get next to Pete.

"First step," Andrew says. "He has to know who you are."

"True. I met him once, over a year ago. He doesn't know I exist."

"Change that."

I begin moseying around the MGM Grand and hanging around the studio during Pete's show. To my surprise, he does recognize me. He waves. I wave back. During the first commercial break, I head over to him and we shake hands.

"Hey, Pete, how's it going?"

"Not bad, Bricker. You okay?"

Bricker. First person who's ever called me that. I like it.

"I'm good, Pete, thanks. Doing those overnights, midnight to five."

"Brutal. Don't know how you do that."

"It takes a certain mentality, I will say that."

"That's for sure. I'd say you have to be a little *different*. Excuse me."

He beckons to a young man in his early twenties standing a few feet to the side. The kid rushes over and Pete peels off a half inch of bills, hundreds, I think, from one of three stacks of cash piled neatly—and high—in front of him. I've never seen so much cash in one place in my life. Pete mumbles something to the kid about the two horse in the fifth race. The young man nods and dashes into the sports book.

Pete looks at me and grins. "Having a big day, Bricker. Feeling good. And it's early. You into the horses?"

"No. I don't gamble."

"You must have other vices."

"Only a couple."

Pete laughs, puts on his headset, says something to his producer who's sitting next to him, and goes back on the air. I wave and head out. I don't want to overstay my welcome, especially since his cohost, the guy on Pete's other side, the guy I'd love to replace, lasers me with the kind of stare a homicide detective would give a suspected murderer.

⸺

Andrew and I increase our calls from twice a week to three or four times a week to almost every day. We become confidants in all things. We usually begin discussing business and then segue into the highs and lows of our personal lives. We offer each other advice. We laugh, we bitch, we analyze, we gossip, we commiserate. We also talk sports. We are both, at heart, the truest of sports fans. We lobby blindly and passionately for our own hometown heroes. I hit him with take after take about the excellence of Patrick Ewing, the majesty of Thurman Munson, the consistency of Derek Jeter. No matter which player I extol, Andrew always shouts me down, declaiming the perfection of Brett Favre. In a way, our nearly daily sports conversations mirror the best segments of my talk show.

One morning I receive a frantic phone call from Charlie Barker, who calls me early enough to wake me.

"I'm in a pinch," he says. "Pete's cohost called in sick."

I sit straight up, blink away my sleep haze, don't even let him finish.

"I'll be there in an hour," I say.

Fifteen minutes before we hit air, I slide into the chair next to Pete Rose. He nods at me and smiles. "Hey, Bricker."

"Hey, Pete. I'm with you today."

"Are you? Good. That's great."

"Excellent. So, what do you want to talk about?"

"No idea."

He rests one hand over all three piles of the hundreds in front of him and flips a page of the *Racing Form* with the other.

"Tell you what," I say. "You lead, I'll follow. I'm just here to make you look good."

Pete turns to me, lifts an eyebrow. "We're gonna do all right," he says.

We click. The moment the show starts, Pete and I fall into an easy flow. I have a sense of leading him exactly where he wants to go, right into his comfort zone. He's focused and funny and incredibly knowledgeable. The producer feeds us one guest, a retired baseball player. Pete's never met him, but within seconds Pete's schmoozing with him like he's an old friend. After the first hour, we go to a break. Pete removes his headset and swats me on the back. "Nice job, Bricker. We're a good team."

"You make it easy," I say.

"Hey," he calls over to the producer. "Who we got lined up for the next segment?"

The producer goes pale. "Um. Nobody."

Pete scribbles two phone numbers on the front page of the *Racing Form*. "Bricker, call these two numbers. Start with Henry. If he don't pick up, call Nolan."

I dial the first number, get an answering machine. As a deep voice invites me to leave a message, I realize, *That's Henry Aaron. I'm about to leave a message for Hammering Hank Aaron, the greatest home run hitter in the history of baseball.*

I click off.

"He there?" Pete says.

"No. I got the answering machine."

"Try Nolan."

I nod, and in a few seconds I'm on the line with Nolan Ryan. "Mr. Ryan, this is JT. I'm on the radio with Pete Rose. Do you have a minute to come on the show?"

"Sure," Nolan Ryan says. "Anything for Pete."

We come out of the break and I bring Nolan Ryan on with Pete, and even though I'm part of the conversation I drift away.

For a few moments I become a listener, and what I hear is Pete Rose and Nolan Ryan talking baseball as if they're in a sports bar, or better, in a dugout. Radio gold.

Two hours with Pete Rose and I'm on a mission.

I need to become Pete's partner and not just for today.

—

Andrew hears part of my show with Pete and feels as stoked as I am. "Beautiful job, JT. You guys had chemistry."

"Yeah, I felt that, too."

"Hey, babe, when it comes to Pete Rose, we got something in common. A few years ago, when I was on the air, I did some time with Pete. We did a midday show in Florida, from the Pete Rose Cafe. Didn't last long. We both moved on."

"Wow." I'm about to ask Andrew if Pete would remember him, but I stop myself. I have a feeling that everyone remembers Andrew.

"You gotta get yourself in there somehow, full-time," Andrew says.

"I know. Any ideas how?"

"I already said something. At least you got one good review."

We consider a couple of approaches. None feels right.

"There's only one way," I say. "The squeaky wheel."

Andrew clucks once as he mulls this over. "Risky," he says.

"What's the risk?"

"That you'll become an annoying asshole."

"Never stopped me before," I say.

I drop by Charlie's office unannounced. I arrive around noon, the same time that Pete's show starts. I plan this so Charlie can see my face and simultaneously listen to Pete and his partner, the guy I want to replace, the guy I *will* replace because I'm better than he is. I know it and Charlie knows it.

"I need to cohost with Pete again," I say.

"I hear you," he says.

"I want to be on with Pete full-time. I'm better than what you got."

"Maybe so. It's just not that easy."

"I'm gonna come back every day until you give me the gig."

"Please don't do that."

"I can't help myself," I say.

"JT, I know you want to be on with Pete. I get it. I can't do it yet."

"See you tomorrow," I say.

I stop by Charlie's office every day on my way to lunch at the $1.99 buffet at Ellis Island. On certain days, I hear Andrew's voice warning me that Charlie will find me an annoying asshole. On other days, Charlie heaves a sigh when he sees my half-moon grin and waves me in. On those days I can't tell if Charlie thinks I'm crazy, driven, or a freak. I want to believe that he admires my ambition and tenacity. It doesn't much matter. I truly can't help myself. Once I fixate on something, I won't let it go until I get it. I'm like a rottweiler with a rawhide bone. Meanwhile, Andrew confides in me that he's hearing rumblings of a shake-up at the Sports Fan Radio Network.

"Nothing specific," he says. "Just rumors that they're gonna start shuffling people around."

"People like Pete's cohost?"

"Don't know. Lotta movement all over, I'm hearing. Far as Pete's cohost, don't get your hopes too high, but it's possible."

"You know something."

"Nothing specific. But—"

"Yeah?"

"Make sure you drop in tomorrow."

The next morning when I stop in to see Charlie, he rolls his eyes, shakes his head, and signals me to come in and close the door. "Take a seat."

"I'm too nervous," I say.

"Fine. Stand. We're changing the lineup a bit."

"Meaning?"

"You got *The Pete Rose Show*."

I bang my hand on his desk.

"*Yes!* Thank you, Charlie."

"Oh, is that something you'd like to do?"

We laugh.

"This is unbelievable," I say. "The Bricker and Pete. I'm pinching myself. I would do this gig for free."

"Good, because I can't pay you."

"You serious?"

"I run a sports talk radio network. I haven't laughed since 1985."

"So, I guess I don't have much wiggle room, huh?"

"None."

"I said I'd do it for free. I didn't mean it at the time. But I do now."

We shake hands.

———

My workdays now border on the maniacal. Every night, midnight to five a.m., I blast forth from *The Brickhouse*—the wild Bobby Machado at the controls running the show—leading off with and belting out my monologue, slamming phone calls, bantering with a few guests, speeding, wailing, blasting, a total rush of five-hour energy. Spent, I head home, crash, grab a couple hours of sleep, check in with Andrew, freshen up, and power over to the MGM Grand to cohost *The Pete Rose Show*. In the afternoon, winding down from my—count them—seven hours on the air, I often check in with Andrew again. In between heated conversations about radio, sports, and our social lives—we both party hard and often, he in South Beach, me on the Las Vegas Strip—we plot my next move: how to get paid.

Andrew provides a storehouse of information and educated opinion, offering power ratings for all the players in radio, on air, and behind the scenes. I start by taking notes on one of my trusty legal pads, but staring at the names I've written, the cross outs, the connectors, I realize I need more color and more surface space. I haul out the Las Vegas yellow pages, look up the closest office supply store, head over, and purchase a couple of sheets of oak tag. Just as I created a poster's worth of information to create my early shows in Southern California, I now begin creating a chart for the sports talk radio business.

I put Jim Rome in the center and, based on the buzz I hear from Andrew and others at Sports Fan Radio, I add these other major players: the Fabulous Sports Babe, Hacksaw, Mike and the Mad Dog (the kings of New York), Mike North (from Chicago, self-proclaimed Monster of the Midway), and the up-and-coming, insane, and supremely talented Scott Ferrall, who burns hotter and with even more energy than I have.

I write down the stations and networks where they work, the audience they reach, their salaries—based on Andrew's educated estimates—and add what I consider the most significant piece of the puzzle: their agents.

When I finish the poster, I tape it to the wall, stare at it, and study it. At first, unblinking, my gaze boring into the poster, I feel nothing but frustration. Looking at the names I've written, I know that I work longer and harder than all of them, and that I make way less than any of them. Hell, compared to almost anyone in almost any business, my salary is a joke.

And then my self-pity melts away, kicked aside by my ambition.

Why did I really make the poster?

Because I want to be on it.

—

I want to be ready before I ask for Andrew's help, so I bide my time for several months. By then, I've got Vegas wired. I pour my heart and soul into my night show, grab enough sleep to refresh myself for Pete Rose, get home and catch a little more sleep, grab dinner and hang out at the Hard Rock with Todd and the boys weeknights, and paint the town with them every weekend. While I love the Vegas nightlife, my main focus stays on doing my shows. As I bank each one, I can tell that I'm getting better.

One day I decide to pop the question to Andrew. He beats me to it.

"I've been thinking about something," he says.

"Okay," I say, "and then I want to talk to you about something."

"You need an agent," he says.

"Uncanny," I say. "That's exactly what I want to ask you about."

"Crazy."

"I know."

"You got anybody in mind?"

"I do," I say, peering at the poster. "I've been doing some research, and I see that Miller Broadcast Management out of Chicago seems to handle a lot of big names."

"Lisa and Matt Miller," Andrew says. "They're really good. They're friends of mine."

"What are they, husband and wife?"

"Mother and son. They're a trip. I'll call them for you. Pave the way."

He does. I wait a few days, call them, and thanks to Andrew's introduction, Lisa gets right on the line. We talk for a few minutes, and words such as *talent* and *potential* float in the air. Even though Lisa says they're not taking on any new clients, she agrees to listen to my tape as a favor to Andrew.

After I thank her and hang up, I call Andrew immediately.

For the first time, he doesn't take my call. An assistant at the radio station tells me he's in a meeting. I don't hear from him the rest of the day. As I prepare to head over to the Hard Rock, I get a phone call. Andrew.

"Yeah, babe."

"Hey, how you doing? Everything all right?"

"Everything's good. Real good." A pause. "I'm outta here in Miami."

"Whoa."

"Moving to San Antonio. Major opportunity. I'm gonna run the flagship station for Clear Channel, WOAI."

"The Ticket 760," I say.

Andrew laughs. "You're good."

"I soak all this shit up. Plus I had a great teacher."

"Oh, yeah!"

"So when do you start?"

"Yesterday. Gotta pack up and move out. Soon as I get settled, I'll call you. I'm gonna have you come down. Weird, huh, that we've never met in person?"

"A little bit."

"That will change."

"The Ticket in San Antonio, huh? Rome talks about that station all the time. Talks about the program director. Well, the old one. Tells his clones, you gotta bang your monkey."

"Believe me, I know. Once I get there, he'll be telling them to bang your *gorilla*. He already started."

"A big step," I say.

"That's the thing about radio," Andrew says. "Don't nail anything down in your apartment because you're probably gonna move."

"No built-in bookcases."

"Hell, no."

"Awright," I say. "We'll talk."

"Bet on it," Andrew says.

Andrew takes some time to settle into San Antonio. He finds a spacious house in the suburbs, furnishes it, and we go back to speaking every morning, every afternoon, and sometimes in the evenings.

One day I get a phone call from Lisa Miller of Miller Broadcast Management.

She liked the tape. She puts her son, Matt, on the line. They've decided to take me on as a client. Lisa informs me that my days of working for free have come to an end.

Within weeks, she's on the phone with the same business guy who got me to come to Vegas for $27,500 a year.

She tells him that she is my agent and she wants to renegotiate my deal.

He has a contract, the business guy says.

Tear it up, Lisa says.

What if I say no? the business guy says.

Then you'll have to find somebody else to do overnights and work with Pete Rose.

Lisa calls me a week later to tell me I have a new contract with the Sports Fan Radio Network.

I will be making six figures a year.

8.

Start Me Up

"I'M FLYING YOU OUT."

Early November.

Not only has Andrew settled in at WOAI, thanks to Jim Rome's constant haranguing of his clones in San Antonio to "bang their gorilla," Andrew has become famous, at least as famous as a sports talk radio program director can become. When it comes to Rome, Andrew has put his onions on the line and built his lineup around him, programming the rock star of sports talk twice a day—mornings and replaying his show at night. Andrew decides to bring Rome to San Antonio, along with sports talk's most volatile voice, Scott Ferrall, and me, the new kid, who does more live talk radio than anybody in the country.

"Every year the station hosts a well-known charity event during the run-up to Christmas called Elf Louise," Andrew says. "Very cool event. We raise money to buy gifts for needy kids. We have a radiothon. It'll be Rome, Ferrall, and you."

I'm honored but not surprised. Andrew and I talk constantly and have become closer than ever. Between him and the Millers, I feel as if I've finally broken through the obscurity of overnights and made at least a small dent in the sports talk radio landscape.

"This will rock. I just gotta book a hotel—"

"Out of the question," Andrew says. "You're staying with me."

"You sure?"

"Positive. No discussion. I'll pick you up at the airport."

"Okay, great, thanks. I'll be the guy in the Knicks shirt and Yankees cap looking confused."

Andrew laughs.

"And other than the guy wearing the Packers cap, how will I know you?" I say.

"Oh," he says. "You can't miss me."

———

I stand curbside, craning my neck over taxis and rental shuttles, looking for a car that has pulled over with a guy behind the wheel I imagine being Andrew. No sign so far. I lean against a concrete pillar, adjust the brim of my Yankees cap, and wait.

An SUV the size of a small building on wheels, rock music blaring through the narrow opening in the passenger-side window, eases up to the curb and stops. The driver's door swings open and a huge man with a light brown rabbinical beard and long flowing bleached blond hair strides toward me. He looks like Uncle Buck crossed with Grizzly Adams, only bigger. A smile burns across his face. "JT!" He opens his arms and wraps them around me in a massive hug. "Yeah, babe!"

"Andrew."

I throw my arms around him. I have no choice. We wham each other on the back, pull away, step back, and look each other. His smile never fades. "Good flight?"

"Great, fine, no problems."

"Terrific. And that will be the end of the small talk."

He grabs my suitcase and tosses it into the back of the SUV. I settle into the passenger seat, strap on my seat belt. Andrew watches me, his smile still flashing on high beams. "There's something you need to know about me," he says. "It's kind of important."

Uh-oh, I think.

"Okay," I say.

"I like to eat."

———

Before arriving at his house, we make a Costco run. Andrew loads the oversize shopping cart to overflowing as if he owns a restaurant—cases of beer, packages of steaks, bratwurst, and ready-to-eat chicken wings, bags of potato chips and nachos, flour and corn tortillas, tubs of guacamole, a giant bottle of hot sauce, hunks of cheese, industrial-size bottles of gin, scotch, bourbon, and vermouth, cans of Bloody Mary mix, bottles of wine, and, to be healthy, a couple of bunches of bananas. I whip out my credit card to pay, but Andrew beats me to it, slapping down a platinum card of his own. "You're my guest," he says.

We fill the back of the SUV with our provisions and head to his ranch-style house, spacious and lived in, a showroom of overstuffed leather chairs and couches, high-end sound system, and several wide-screen TVs. I feel as if I've entered a sports bar or state-of-the-art man cave. Andrew shows me to the guest bedroom, where I stash my suitcase and then we head into the kitchen, where he cranks up some classic rock—Journey, Foreigner, and in honor of me, Billy Joel's "New York State of Mind"—and then we dive into a weekend that except for the few hours I spend on the radio doing my show and attending the Elf Louise benefit event with Andrew, Rome, and Ferrall, consists of wall-to-wall eating, drinking, sports watching, and high octane partying with a parade of people Andrew knows and women he's just met, many of whom look like they've just stepped off a model's runway.

"How do you do it?" I ask him late one night or early one morning as the latest beauty unfolds herself from his side and scurries off to mix him a drink.

He laughs, and then winks. "I have a big heart," he says.

The two days rip by in the kind of debauchery, alcoholic buzz, and time muddle that I haven't enjoyed since many memorable lost weekends at college. At one point Andrew lifts himself off one of the leather sofas and announces, "JT, time for the grand tour," and before I know what's happening, the two of us are in the SUV, heading downtown.

"First stop," Andrew says, pointing to a large turn of the century Southern mansion across the street from the Alamo. "The famous Menger Hotel."

We hand the keys of the SUV to a red-jacketed valet who greets Andrew like a cousin—Andrew seems to know *everybody* in the city, from parking attendants to grocery store cashiers to the top brass at Clear Channel—and head into the lobby, decorated in shades of swimming-pool blue, and then duck into the dark-wood bar, where according to legend and the ancient, crusty bartender who may have been behind the bar at the time, Teddy Roosevelt recruited the Rough Riders. After the Menger, we stroll down River Walk and board a pontoon boat for a lazy ride on the river. Finally, Sunday afternoon, Andrew returns me to the airport for my flight back to Las Vegas. This time we hug like the long-lost brothers we've become.

—

Now, more than ever, the phone becomes my lifeline. On my show, the lines blaze and blink, my regular callers, colorful characters such as the Mayor of Poway, Butch from the Cape, and Benny Jet, waiting on hold to bellow their opinions and connect to my voice and to one another—cabdrivers, bar owners, truck drivers, traveling salesmen, prison guards on their way to the job or heading home, and dozens of others, all night riders who, like me, work the graveyard shift. When I'm off the air, I call my parents in New York, missing them and the rest of my extended family, wondering sometimes why I left the comfort of Long Island and what might have been a safe, secure, *normal* life in favor of the insanity of Las Vegas and the uncertainty of a life on the radio. I phone my friends in San Diego regularly, too, Jimmy, Bobby G., JD. We plot upcoming road trips and inform each other of any and all action in our personal lives and careers. I devote myself to staying connected, to not allowing these relationships to drift, lose momentum, or fray. I use the phone as an extension of myself. These conversations fuel my relationships. Other than the few times we see each other on weekends, they're all we have, the only way I can connect.

Andrew becomes a key player in my phone call rotation. Without ever discussing it or planning it, we call each other every day at lunchtime, a twenty-minute check-in, at minimum. We often speak earlier or in the evening as well, but we never miss a noon call. We meet again in person at the Super Bowl in New Orleans, at Radio Row, a gathering near the Superdome where many of the country's top sports talk hosts convene in a kind of informal convention the week before the game. Andrew serves as host of Radio Row, embracing, literally, every on-air personality, program director, and radio dignitary as warmly as a beloved family member. In the evening, at the restaurant bar of his choice and at the after party in his hotel suite, the celebration continues, as it always does, with an abundance of food, drink, women, and laughter. Andrew is at once the most informed, insightful, and entertaining person I know. His presence—his sheer joy of being, his life force—could fill a stadium.

I tick off the early months of 1997, and then a new feeling of restlessness starts to race through me. I'm on the air five hours every night and two hours every day with Pete Rose, and it's not enough. I want more. I feel that my career isn't moving fast enough. I try to see where all these hours on the air will eventually lead me, but I can't imagine anything ahead except for more late-night hours and what I feel is a kind of obscurity. I talk to Andrew about this. More accurately, I hammer Andrew relentlessly about how I feel.

"I don't think anybody appreciates what I do, the hours I put in, or how good I am," I wail, a refrain that spills out of my mouth with more and more frequency and urgency.

"What do you want?" Andrew asks me. "You want morning drive, you want afternoon drive? You want to replace Mike and the Mad Dog?"

"I just want people to know who I am," I moan.

"They do. They will."

"And yeah, if I had the chance, I would consider morning or afternoon drive."

"You didn't ask me, but I'm about to give you some advice. These are the three most important words in radio. Live by them."

"Hit me."

"Keep your seat."

I let the words sink in.

Andrew continues. "Radio is all about real estate. Right now, you own some prime real estate, all night, every night. It's yours. Nobody else has it. Think long and hard before you give it up. Until then, hold on to it with a death grip. Do nothing to lose it. Because if you do, you'll never get it back."

"Keep the seat," I say, and then I repeat the words because I know Andrew is not giving me advice, he is teaching me a life lesson.

Keep the seat.

Once a month, it seems, the boxing world descends on the Strip with a fury as every major fight and fighter arrives with a hungry entourage ready to tear off a piece of what has become *the* white-hot entertainment capital of the world. As an exclamation point, Mike Tyson, the most notorious boxer the world has ever seen, relocates to Las Vegas. Smart move. Now, for Tyson, every fight becomes a home game.

I hold a longtime fascination with Mike Tyson. I see him as not just a brutal knockout king but as an underdog, a kid who fell into a career with no formal training and had to figure it all out himself, driven by a ferocious work ethic, relentless in the ring, a renegade brawler who will do anything to win. I identify with him. I see my rise in radio as similar to his rise in boxing. I've followed Tyson for years. When I worked at J.T. Moran, during a night of particular decadence, a group of us rented a helicopter and, raising champagne flutes in our thousand-dollar suits, flew from Connecticut to Atlantic City to see Tyson demolish the then undefeated Michael Spinks in what I called the Massacre on the Boardwalk.

Now, in Vegas, on June 28, 1997, Tyson will fight Evander Holyfield at the MGM Grand—where I broadcast my show—in what has been billed the Sound and the Fury. Tyson and Holyfield are fighting for the second time. Holyfield previously dominated Tyson, pummeling him for fifteen rounds, scoring a technical knockout. Tyson and the boxing world have been clamoring for a rematch and Holyfield has obliged. This time Tyson will exact revenge. I'm certain of it. Of course, I don't know him, have never met him, but I feel as if I have a touch of Tyson inside me and I know he's out for blood. I will not miss this fight. I pull my one good suit out of mothballs and arrange for a press pass that puts me ringside, close enough to hear the pop of each jab and dodge droplets of the fighters' sweat.

I roll in early enough before the fight to wind my way through throngs of people to the lounge at the MGM, where the bartender, a guy I know, pours me a preflight cocktail. I sip my drink, swivel on the bar stool, and face the front of the bar as the crowd pours into the hotel lobby. Right away, I feel it, a crackle of aggressive energy that burns up every inch of space inside the MGM. This energy throws me off, fills me with a low-level thrum of fear, the impulse you feel if you get lost very late at night in the wrong neighborhood and your car suddenly dies. Right now I feel that same uncomfortable sensation blinking in my brain like a warning light, leaving my mouth dry as the desert outside. Psychologists have a word for this: *dread*.

More people arrive for the fight. Too many people. The women look dressed for a formal evening out, more like for the opera or a state dinner than a boxing match. The men all look like they're in uniform, expensive tailored black suits as if they're attending a politician's funeral. All of these beautifully dressed people cram into the lobby, jockeying for space. They don't look happy or excited; they look dangerous. If I squint, I swear I can make out the outlines of guns bulging inside the chests of the men's suit coats. I feel as if I'm on the sidelines and about to witness some kind of human explosion.

I finish my drink and weave through the traffic. I stop at our makeshift studio in the sports book and check in with Steve Cofield, the weekend host on the night shift. Steve feels it, too, this twisted electrical undercurrent of dread. I tell him I'm going inside the arena to see the fight. We agree that when the fight concludes, I'll come on the air with him and give him, literally, the blow by blow.

I enter the arena and walk down the aisle to my seat, every step sending me deeper into a black hole of discomfort. All around me people are screaming, shoving, threatening each other. An image of a Looney Tunes cartoon pops into my head, Wile E. Coyote lighting a fuse, then standing aside watching and waiting, hands over his ears, as a blue flame snakes and sizzles toward a run-down shack inside which the Road Runner lies shackled by a dozen sticks of dynamite. That's how I feel: that the arena—the shack—is about to blow.

The fighters enter the ring, and from the beginning I see that Tyson looks unhinged. He circles the ring slowly, his eyes flickering a vicious yellow. The bell rings and the legendary fight begins, Holyfield throwing roundhouse punches, Tyson flailing back, grabbing Evander in a death clinch, and infamously biting both of Holyfield's ears. The referee, Mills Lane, stops the fight, disqualifies Tyson, and Mike, enraged, goes after anything that moves. The crowd, unsatisfied, crazy, feeling ripped off, turns ballistic. They've come as witnesses to an execution and have been told to go home. The execution's been called off. They paid for fifteen rounds of blood and their thirst for vicarious violence still runs hot and unfulfilled. They want what they came for, if not in the ring then in the stands. They attack one another. Brawls break out everywhere. A woman falls and slides face-first down a section of the bleachers. People flee up the aisles, tripping, falling, crawling for the exits. Some form small gangs, hold their ground, and start throwing punches at random people around them. I stand at my seat, find all the exits blocked, and turn back to look inside the ring. Tyson has moved across the ring and is standing in front of me. Our eyes meet. He says nothing, but we lock into each other, a part of his soul melting into mine. He raises his gloved fist in front of his face, waves it slowly, breaks away, and, on the other side of the ring, ducks through the ropes.

I need to get out of here.

I somehow squirm and twist and push my way through the crowd and out of the arena. I race to the studio and sit down next to Steve Cofield. I put on a headset to dull the screaming I hear everywhere. All around us, people rush through the sports book, charge into the casino.

"What happened in there, JT?" Steve asks me on the air.

"Tyson bit Holyfield's *ears*," I say, breathless. "He bit him twice. Both ears. They stopped the fight, disqualified Tyson, and everyone went insane. It's a riot now. Totally out of control. A *riot*."

More people run into the sports book. Some come right at us, then streak past, screaming, searching for a way out. An occasional security guard jogs by, looking lost, hands cupped over a walkie-talkie, pleading for instruction and reinforcements. Three women in their twenties, dressed to kill, holding stiletto heels by their flimsy straps, run up to us while we're on the air. They say that they're being chased. They look pale and desperate. They beg us for help. We don't know what to do or say. We are on the air, doing a fucking radio show. On the *air*, across America. I flip off my microphone and gesture frantically for them to hide under the desk. They scramble beneath Steve and me and tuck into fetal positions against our feet. One woman's cold long fingers grab onto my ankle. Four or five thugs in suits, hands patting their sides, walk into the sports book, look around, and stare at us for a five count. One of them says something and nods right at me. Below the desk, the woman's fingernails dig into my ankle. I stifle a scream. One of the gangsters glares, tips his hat, then they all turn and leave.

"Fuck," I say, hoping my microphone is still off.

Steve goes to a break, then spins out of his headset. "We're outta here," he says.

"Come on, girls," I say, bending over. "The coast is clear."

The girls slither out from beneath the desk and sprint out of the sports book, shaken, shouting thanks over their shoulders.

"Side door," I say to Steve. "Left side of the casino."

We run for it, bang our shoulders into the outside door. A second before I hit the street, a roar from the casino catches my attention. I turn back and see two guys in suits turning over a blackjack table.

I decompress at the Hard Rock's center bar, nursing a vodka and 7UP across from Todd. I hold court, recounting the riot I witnessed at the MGM Grand and reported on the radio. Patrons of the bar listen, rapt. I feel as if I'm doing a special edition of my talk show. Todd pours drinks and takes in my story, mesmerized. Finally, around three a.m., a wave of exhaustion hitting me, I head out into the stifling night air and stagger back to my apartment.

The next day Todd calls me to tell me that at the end of his shift, at five a.m., on a whim, he decided to drive by Mike Tyson's mansion, which, as he and all the bartenders in town know, looms tucked away on the outskirts of the city, hidden behind wrought-iron gates. As Todd came up Tyson's street, the gates to the mansion rumbled and spread apart, and Mike Tyson, shirtless, his eyes narrow and dark, roared out of the driveway on his motorcycle and rode blindly into the desert.

January 25, 1998.

Crunched inside a huddle of green-shirt-wearing, fist-pumping, semi-inebriated fans from Wisconsin, Andrew and I sit in the club level of Qualcomm Stadium in San Diego, watching his beloved Green Bay Packers take on the Denver Broncos in Super Bowl XXXII. We pound shots of tequila and chase them with beers, Andrew's thirst spiked by his nervous gorging of the record-breaking amount of chips and dip he's gouged out of a nearby glass bowl the size and shape of an upside-down lamp shade. Wired, Andrew can't sit still for five seconds. He stands, plows through the huddle of fans, runs his fingers through his rock star's flowing locks, returns, downs a shot of tequila, pours another, turns and gazes miserably at the 50-yard line as the singing group Boyz II Men launches into a medley of R&B songs, their contribution to the Forty-Year Tribute to Motown halftime entertainment.

Andrew gestures toward the field with his shot glass. "I'm a fucking wreck."

"Why? You're *up*," I say, knocking back the rest of my beer, tilting the neck of the empty at the scoreboard below showing the Packers leading the Broncos 17–14 at the half.

"I got a bad feeling," he says. "They look gassed."

I shrug and wrestle another beer out of an ice chest at the edge of the couch a few feet away.

"I've done research," Andrew says. "In winter, teams that come to Southern California from the Midwest always lose. The Big Ten never wins the Rose Bowl. It's not that the Pac Ten is better. It's because the Big Ten teams don't do warm weather."

"*College* teams," I say, drawing on my beer.

Andrew begins to pace. He starts to speak, his voice rising, his hands flying, gesturing, fingers rotating, pointing, fists clenching. Andrew is the most animated speaker I've ever known. "It's a *fact*. The players' blood thins out in the cold weather. The capillaries either shrink or expand, I forget which, plus I'm *drunk*, but the idea is that it takes more physical *effort* for my guys from Wisconsin, my Packers, to *deal* with the heat and shit. Look it up. I'm not making this up. It's fucking *science*."

His point made, clumsily but emphatically, he sways, tipping slightly in the direction of the 50-yard line. "Holmgren should've flown them out earlier," he mutters.

I shake my head. "I'm glad you're ahead. Otherwise you might be crazy."

This allows Andrew a smile. "Let's just say I'm concerned." He stretches his arms out. "I'm concerned for all of us."

In the end, Andrew has reason to be concerned. In a back-and-forth grind-out game, Denver beats Green Bay, 31–24.

Andrew's shoulders sag beneath the mountain of grief he, a diehard lifetime Packer fan, feels after the loss. The grief is genuine and deep; for Andrew, nothing is put on or part of a character he plays. He bleeds Packer green the way I bleed Knicks, Yankees, and Giants blue. Outside the stadium, we roll into the backseat of a limo, courtesy of Clear Channel, and stare silently out our respective windows as the car pulls away from Qualcomm. I want to console him. I want to tell him, "Hey, man, at least the Packers got to the Super Bowl. That's awesome. You came in second in the *world*," but I keep quiet because I know that's not what he wants to hear.

"We came so close," Andrew says, finally. "That's what hurts the most."

—

Two weeks later, Andrew calls me late one afternoon: surprising, because an afternoon call is not part of our usual rotation unless something is up. He speaks quickly and sounds breathless from excitement. "Yeah, *babe*. You sitting down?"

"I am."

"My buddy Bill Scull just sent me two tickets to see the Rolling Stones at the Hard Rock on Valentine's Day. Right in your backyard."

"That's freaking awesome. This is the concert of the year. They're playing in this really small theater. It's gonna be like a private show."

"Cool. You're gonna love it."

"Me?"

"Yeah. I'm not going."

"Really? You sure?"

"First, I can't go, I got too much on my plate. Second, I don't really love Vegas. Third, I don't really love the Stones. I'll FedEx the ducats to you soon as we hang up."

"Wow. Thanks, man. How much do I owe you?"

"No money exchanges hands here. We're comped. You won't believe these seats. Right up front. Any closer and Mick's giving you a lap dance. Later."

⁓

Normally, I'd give Jimmy B. first crack, but he's heading to Seattle on business—he's landed a new gig and life is good—so I call Bobby G. I know he'll be stoked. I'm right. He goes out of his mind. "Holy shit! The Stones at the Hard Rock? That's the biggest concert in America."

"Got two tickets. Awesome seats. Call JD. You guys gotta get out here for this."

"Hold up. You said you got *two* tickets."

"Yeah, I do. Don't worry. We'll figure it out. Just get out here."

"Oh, we will," Bobby G. says. "Figure it out."

⁓

Walking into the Hard Rock, flanked by JD Crow and Bobby G., I feel as if I'm floating. We blow through the lobby, cross into the casino, and head toward the center bar, eyes front and focused, passing scores of people, all of whom seem to be moving in slow motion. The air crackles, hot, electric, but different from what I felt months ago at the MGM Grand before the Tyson fight. This night I feel pops of anticipation. I can't articulate it, but this night I have no feeling of dread. I feel instead that something's coming.

We can't get near the center bar. A cluster of people backed up four and five deep stand jammed together, pushing in a scrum toward Todd and the other bartenders I hang with, Chris and Little Dave, who are taking drink orders and pouring cocktails and shots in one single fluid motion without looking up, the bottles extensions of their arms. I stop at the bottom of the two stairs leading up to the center bar and wait for Todd to catch my eye. He does, finally, in midpour, nods, and even though he and the other guys are buried, he slices the air in front of him in a karate chop motion, and somehow the cluster of people divides—the sea of humanity at the Hard Rock Cafe center bar parts—and JD, Bobby G., and I make our way up to the bar. We don't order. We don't have to. Todd slides three vodka and 7UPs in front of us.

"Gonna be some night," Todd says.

"Unreal," I say.

"Hottest concert in the country," Todd says. "How'd you get tickets?"

"Andrew." Todd smiles as if to say, *Of course*. He has never met Andrew but he knows Andrew because of how often I talk about him. "Andrew didn't want to go so he handed them off to me," I say, cooling my hand on my drink.

Someone shouts, "To a great night!" and Bobby G., JD,

and I throw down our drinks and slam our empty glasses onto the bar at the same time. Todd grins and in thirty seconds three more drinks materialize in front of us. I slap five with Todd and lean down to hear something JD says, nearly impossible in this crunch of people. The mixture of cigarette smoke and strong perfume stings my eyes, the Stones wail on tape over the hotel's loudspeakers, and the volume of the music and the warmth of the booze cause my stomach to rumble. I turn to see if Bobby G. has settled in and instead see clamped onto his arm a blonde who's falling out of her dress. He laughs, lowers his head, and a second blonde appears on his other side, her long fake pink fingernails curled around Bobby's biceps. He says something and the two blondes laugh hysterically. I decide that they are already drunk and without tickets.

"Here we go," I say to JD, who scans each blonde from head to toe and then shakes his head reverentially.

"How does he do it?" he says.

"Balls," I say. "Dude's got balls."

"Not that I'm worried," JD says, "but how are we all gonna get in? I'm not great in math, but I count three of us and two tickets."

Bobby's face appears in front of us, blocking both blondes. "Not a problem."

And then his face flies out of view, as if yanked by a string.

JD laughs, moves a step over to grab another drink. I lean back and someone gently jostles me, nudging me in the back. I'm not sure why, but I'm compelled to turn around.

And there she is.

Blonde, tall, striking, wearing a wild animal print jacket, black pants, and heels.

A presence.

I know it's not possible, I know I've seen too many movies, but I swear she's bathed in light.

"Hi," I say.

"Hello."

An hour passes.

Feels like it anyway.

"Sorry." She tilts the big blonde hair toward the bar. "That's my drink."

I reach over and hand it to her. "You wouldn't happen to be alone?" I say.

"I would. As a matter of fact."

I inch to my left, make room. "Slide in."

She steps forward and fills in the space next to me.

My pulse quickens. My legs feel rubbery. I press my palms into the bar to steady myself. Suddenly I have no sense of JD or Bobby G. or their blondes even existing. They have evaporated. This woman seems to be the only person in the entire room.

"How you doing?" I say, and wince at those words bouncing back at me and clattering in my head, in what I instantly identify as the lamest line I've ever uttered.

"I'm good."

"You got a ticket to the show? Or just checking out the scene?"

She looks me over, assesses me in an *is this guy for real* gaze.

"Yes." A sip of her drink. "I have a ticket. I have to pick it up at will call." She pauses, sips. "I won it in a raffle. I've been thinking that tonight's my lucky night."

She looks away when she says this but I feel myself blush. "John," I say.

She turns and faces me. "Julie."

"Are you from here?"

"I work here. I'm a teacher. I'm from Illinois."

"Did you go to Illinois?"

"I did."

"The Fighting Illini," I say.

She nods. "Correct. Where did you go to school?"

"Geneseo State."

"Wow." She sips her drink. "Never heard of it."

I laugh. She holds for a second and laughs with me. We don't say anything for the next twenty seconds, mainly because I'm trying to fight an overwhelming urge to kiss her. I swallow and blurt, "So, you're going to the concert for free?"

"No," Julie says. "I have to pay. I won the *right* to buy a ticket."

"At least you got in," I say.

"Yeah, well, it's not a great seat. It's in the balcony. But I don't care."

"Sure. I mean, it's the Stones."

"Actually, my mom's the one who got me to enter the raffle." Julie reddens, rims her drink glass with a finger. "I have no idea why I'm telling you all this."

"It's important information," I say.

"It's key."

I look into her eyes. She doesn't waver, doesn't blink. I feel as if I've fallen into a soft green pool of light.

Probably too early to tell her I'm in love with her.

"Yo, JT," Bobby says, the blondes attached to him like barnacles. "We better make our move."

"Huh?" I say. "Oh. Yes. Yeah."

Bobby leans across the bar, scans Julie. She ducks her head, drills her look back into my eyes. "Well, John, I better go get my ticket."

"I'll go with you," I say.

"Um, just…" Bobby stretches past blonde number two and whispers into my ear, "We better not split up. It's a fucking zoo. We lose each other, we'll never hook up again."

"Stay here," I say. "I'll be right back. Stay *here*."

The insistence in my voice freezes him. He looks at me, then at Julie, then back at me, then back at Julie. "Bob," he says, offering his hand.

"Julie," she says, accepting his hand, knocking him back with a killer smile.

"I got an idea," Bobby says. "I'll meet you in front of the stage. At our seats. You and JD take the tickets."

I can tell by his half grin that he's just hatched some crazy scheme. Given the crowd and tight security, I'm worried he might be shut out. "Are you sure?"

"In through the out door," Bobby says and winks. He gathers up three cocktails from the bar and whispers something to the blondes. They giggle. Bobby stands and, balancing all three drinks, a blonde clinging to each arm, he steps down from the center bar and heads toward the closest exit. He says something to a hefty security guard, who's guarding the door. The guy laughs, and a second later Bobby and the blondes leave the hotel and disappear into the night.

"Don't move," I say to JD.

Side by side, Julie and I wind our way down the steps from the bar and head over to will call at the far end of the lobby. The line moves fast, and before we know it she's holding her ticket and we're on the perimeter of the center bar. We both crane our necks at people starting to go into the concert, one door leading to the orchestra, the other upstairs to the balcony.

I toe the carpet. I'm suddenly off balance, desperately trying to hold on to this moment as long as I can. I stand in front of Julie, this vision, and for once the king of cold calls goes mute.

"So, this is it," Julie says. "Well. I enjoyed meeting you, John."

"Yeah, no, this was great."

"I better go. They said it's standing room only in the balcony, first come, first served kind of thing."

"I'm in front. First row." I squint up at the ceiling feeling flushed by the second lamest thing I've ever said.

"Okay," Julie says. "Thanks for walking me to will call and for the drink."

She turns to go. I reach for her wrist, miss, grab a handful of air. She must feel my whiff, though, because she turns back. She stands, riveted, waiting for me to do...or say...something.

"I'll come get you," I say.

Her eyes widen and she smiles a little and then she's gone.

I squeeze back through the crowd to the center bar. I slap a big bill on the bar in front of Todd, who pushes it back to me. "Enjoy the show," he says.

I hand JD his ticket. "Let's do this," I say, but as we go into the concert and an usher tears our tickets, hands us the stubs, and we head down the aisle to the very front of the theater, to the very first row, all I can think about is the woman with the big blonde hair in the wild animal print jacket. All I can think about it Julie.

"Wait," JD says, as we edge into the row, sidestepping to our seats, "is that—?"

It is.

Jack Nicholson, and Sting, and Eddie Murphy, and Gene Simmons, and David Spade, and Brad Pitt, and Pamela Anderson all over the newly sober Tommy Lee.

The lights dim and then fade to black. Sheryl Crow, opening for the Stones, walks onstage, waves to the cheering audience, bends down, and says hi to us. We're sitting five feet away. She jumps to her feet, straps on her guitar, and starts her first song just as the footsteps of latecomers pound down the aisle. I look to my left and see Bobby G. and the blondes racing toward us. The blondes veer to the left and Bobby waves at them and then hustles into our row. JD and I laugh as Bobby squeezes by us.

"They're for later," he says.

On the stage, right in front of us, Sheryl Crow finishes her first song and immediately strums the chords leading into her second song. The crowd claps along and I stare at Sheryl Crow. My head feels heavy and buzzed from our preshow cocktail hour, and as I clap along to this familiar song, the crowd mostly on their feet around me, I feel empty.

I can't stop thinking about her.

Julie.

I let her slip away.

I let her walk out of my life.

I can't explain why, I can't define how, but I can't stop thinking that Julie—as crazy as it sounds—is my future.

I become dimly aware of the audience rising as Sheryl Crow crashes a final chord to her second song and goes into her third song, her big hit, "If It Makes You Happy," and everyone in the entire theater stands and rocks and stomps and sings along. I turn to JD and say, "Give me your ticket stub."

He hears me but he doesn't understand. "What?"

"Give me your ticket stub."

He fumbles in his pocket and removes the small crumpled slip of paper. I snatch it out of his hand as if it's on fire, sidestep out of our row, and bolt up the aisle.

I take the stairs to the balcony two at a time and face the crowd.

I stop, momentarily panicked.

How will I find her?

I move three steps in and she fills my sight line. She stands taller than anyone around her, her blonde mane swaying, her hands clapping, her mouth in a tight circle singing, "If it makes you happpppy..."

I power my way through the crowd until I'm standing behind her. I tap her on the shoulder.

She whips around, sees me, and her mouth drops open, then closes in what looks like shock, and then her face breaks into a shy grin.

"Give me your hand," I say.

She doesn't hesitate. She reaches for me. I lead her through the crowd, and as I grip her hand tighter we leave the balcony, practically run down the stairs, into the aisle, the front row, and into our seats.

"I told you I'd come get you," I say.

"I didn't believe you," she says.

She pauses.

"I do now," she says.

—

We dance and sing along to Sheryl Crow, whose half-hour warm-up to the Rolling Stones lights the whole crowd on fire. At some point, I realize that Bobby has disappeared. JD catches my eye and leans across Julie to say, "He got bounced."

"What?"

"Yeah, security asked to see his ticket and when he couldn't deliver, the rent-a-cop escorted him from the arena."

"I feel terrible," Julie says.

"You don't have to worry," I say. "He'll be back. I guarantee it."

The houselights fade and come up immediately, giving us a heads-up that the Stones are a minute away from running onto the stage. The crowd roars, then buzzes, and a cocktail waitress in a skimpy blouse and short, tight skirt wiggles down the aisle carrying a tray aloft with three bottles of champagne. In her wake, a step behind her, Bobby struts, waving at strangers as if he owns the place.

"Right here," Bobby instructs. The waitress stops at our row and Bobby passes a bottle of champagne to me, one to JD, and then he stretches over a couple of people and hands a bottle to Tommy Lee, who grabs it and gives Bobby the thumbs-up while Pamela glowers first at Tommy and then at Bobby G. I tip the waitress, turn back, and see Tommy popping the cork, tilting his head back, guzzling champagne right from the bottle.

"I thought he was on the wagon," JD says.

"Where'd you hear that?" I say.

"*National Enquirer.* I read it in the supermarket."

"The paper of record," I say.

Days later, the tabloids and entertainment gossip media will report that Pamela Anderson has dumped Tommy Lee because of some excessive, out-of-control rock star behavior, which we choose to believe started the moment Bobby G. handed Tommy Lee the bottle of champagne. "We meet again," Bobby says to Julie, sliding by her into the seat next to JD. "Pop that cork."

I do, and an instant later the houselights go down, the crowd explodes, and all of us in the arena leap to our feet. The Rolling Stones burst out of the wings and jog onto the stage, almost as if the sound of the champagne cork popping has served as a starter's pistol. Keith Richards purses his lips and plucks his guitar like a wild man and the band goes into the evocative introduction to "Start Me Up." Charlie Watts is wailing on the drums and then Keith, ripping those familiar jangling chords on his guitar, bounces right over to us, bends over, and reaches down. He's inches away, so close I smell menthol on his breath and cigarette smoke wafting out of every pore. He offers his open hand and Bobby G.—concert crasher—slaps Keith five and toasts him with the champagne bottle. Keith duckwalks backward and Mick howls, "If you start me up, I'll never stop…" Julie, her head wagging, her blonde hair waving in time to the beat, lost in the music, sings, dances, rivulets of sheer joy jumping off her face. I dance with her, my arm locked around her waist. I pull her into me, bump her hip with mine, and in my own private duet with Mick—oh, I'm gone, so gone—join him in the chorus, falling off the plank into Julie's eyes, screaming the words that sum up exactly how I feel about this woman and what I just know our future will bring: *You make a grown man cry.*"

The next morning, as soon as I'm sober and coherent, I call Andrew. I give him the details of the night—the raging Rolling Stones concert, how Bobby G. snuck in without a ticket and handed Tommy Lee that infamous bottle of champagne, and about the celebs rocking out right next to us. But mainly I gush about Julie. "She's it," I tell him. "She's the one."

"Wow. Big news."

"Huge. She's different, Andrew. I can't explain it. And I think she feels the same way about me." I pause. "This may sound weird, but it's like it was meant to be."

"Fate," Andrew says.

"Exactly. You don't give me those tickets, I don't meet her."

"Plus, you're at the bar, boom, there she is. She shows up ten minutes later or five minutes earlier, you miss her. And she's not on the other side of the bar. She's right behind you."

"Destiny," I say. "I'm telling you."

"Still, play it cool. Take your time. You don't want to seem desperate. Wait a few days before you call her."

My voice cracks. "Okay, yeah, good advice."

"Shit. You already called her."

"We're going out tomorrow night."

"You are lost, bro," Andrew says. "Lost."

"Not at all. She's great. I'm into her, but I have this under control."

"Ha! When's the wedding?"

"Yeah. Right."

After our date the following night, Julie and I start seeing each other regularly and calling each other constantly.

Andrew's right.

Within three weeks, Julie and I start talking about marriage.

9.

Voice from the Black Hole

San Francisco
1998–2001

SOME NIGHTS AROUND three a.m., the danger hour, waiting for my second wind, needing a jolt, fearing the show will dissolve into a transcontinental hum, the outlaws call. They are the denizens of the dark and they save me.

Raider Rob, an aggressive, do-rag-wearing, gravelly-voiced screamer, who, according to at least one person, invented Raider Nation, leads the way, railing about his beloved Raiders. Raider Rob, a participant in the talk show since I hit Vegas, calls with epic energy. I happily provide him a forum, allowing as much time as he needs. Bizarre, but Raider Rob reminds me of me.

Raider Rob from the street gives way to Raider Mort, old-school Oakland Raiders fan, ex–college basketball player who, with Raider Rob, forms two sides of a coin. Raider Mort, a retired schoolteacher, former nightclub owner, and real estate maven, is more educated, more polished, but no less passionate.

Raider Rob and Raider Mort pave the way for others in Raiders Nation. I welcome them all, engage them, challenge them, and never disrespect them. And so they call often. I pump their opinions and encourage their excess. I offer them a voice on the radio. I am their champion.

As they call, beefing up my show, giving it edge, I'm unaware of another regular listener who tunes in frequently. He is Bruce Allen, an executive working for the Oakland Raiders, a fan of Raider Mort and Raider Rob and of my show.

I'm also unaware that Bruce Allen and Andrew Ashwood are longtime friends.

One day, as he often does, Bruce calls Andrew, whom he calls Bubba.

"Hey, Bubba," Bruce says. "Got a question for you. I've been listening to this guy on the radio at night, JT the Brick. You know him?"

"Know him?" Andrew laughs. "JT's the *man*."

⁓

September 1998.

It happens fast.

One day, lounging at home while I scribble topics on a legal pad for my nighttime show, the phone rings.

"You sitting down?" Lisa Miller. No hello, no small talk, voice like sandpaper. She doesn't wait for me to answer. "You're going to San Francisco."

"I'm *what*?"

"I got you the pre- and postgame for the Oakland Raiders.

Bruce Allen's apparently a big fan. You can do your night show from there. I'm also working on getting you middays on KNBR 1050, the new home of the Raiders. You love working two shifts, plus weekends, right?"

"I mean, I don't mind it, but—"

"You also won't mind the bump in pay I got you. I know you like working with Pete, so tell him thank you very much, you've been great, it's been real, I'm gonna miss you, and then get your ass to San Francisco."

"Okay, this is, wow, *okay*, when do I start?"

"Yesterday."

—

"San Francisco?"

I sit across from Julie at her kitchen table. Her apartment is sunny and filled with books. The first time Julie brought me here I felt as if I'd wandered into a small local library. Now, more than five months later, I practically live here.

Julie fiddles with a red pen at the table, which is strewn with papers she's been grading. Jittery, she moves her hands constantly, to her face, through her hair. I gently place my hand over hers, interlocking our fingers.

"Nothing's gonna change," I tell her.

She looks at me, blinks as if she's got something in her eye.

"With us," I say.

Maybe she reads some doubt in my eyes, a glimmer of hesitation, because she says with surprising passion, "You have to go. It's a big opportunity."

"I know."

"And you're right. Nothing's gonna change. I'll come up every weekend. Who doesn't love San Francisco, right? The City by the Bay?"

I release her hand, start fiddling with the pen she abandoned. "We're just getting started and you're already a radio widow," I say.

"Tough duty, huh?"

"I warned you about this business. We're always moving or getting fired."

She removes the pen from my hand, closes her hand over mine, and locks her eyes on me. "Get this, JT the Brick. I'm in it for the long haul."

⟋

I stand by the window in Tony Salvador's office, a large corner office that overlooks the city, Fisherman's Wharf below, the Golden Gate Bridge beyond, taking in a view that tourists buy on postcards. As I wait for Mr. Salvador, the general manager of KNBR, and peer out at one of the most breathtaking cities in the world, I say aloud, "You've come a long way from Massapequa."

The door swings open and Tony Salvador, tall, dapper, olive-skinned, a guy who looks as if he's just stepped out of one of the *Godfather* movies, rushes in and shakes my hand. "Hey, Johnny, how you doing?"

"Fine, Mr. Salvador, thank you."

"You settled in? Michelle set you up with an apartment?"

"All set. She's been great."

"How about Bruce? He treating you right?"

"Oh, he's been unbelievable. I can't thank you enough, really, for everything—"

Tony Salvador flicks two fingers through the air as if he's flicking at a fly and gestures for me to sit. I sink into one of two leather chairs in a corner of the office. Tony plops into the other chair, across from me.

Tony taps his lip, then leans into me as if he's about to share a secret. "Johnny," he says. "This is your shot. San Francisco. Top five market. In the country. In the whole *country*. You up for this?"

Now I lean forward. "I was born for this."

"Beautiful. I knew it. You gotta step up and you gotta be ready to go. We got confidence in you. You're gonna be on this station and you're gonna work."

"I'm totally ready."

"I like it. I like it a lot. Welcome aboard, Johnny."

He stands up, indicating the meeting—all twenty seconds of it—is over. I hustle out of my chair, which suddenly hisses, sounding as if I've let all the air out of it, and Tony Salvador again pumps my hand, this time longer, firmer, accompanied by a wide smile. "Don't screw it up," he says.

I never know exactly what part Andrew plays in my move from Las Vegas to San Francisco and being hired by Bruce Allen to host a total of three hours before and after every Oakland Raiders game. But from our twice-daily phone calls, I determine that as the King Kong of Connectors, he may have played various parts at different times—initiator, cheerleader, consultant, reference, friendly nudge, and although I only imagine this role but wouldn't put it past him, puppet master. I'm aware that I can be intense, off the air as well as on, and that when I grab hold of a topic or an idea, I will cling to it, ride it to the ground, beat it to death—or so Andrew has told me—complaining constantly and wailing incessantly, usually about what I see as my stalled momentum. My shock this time is that he *heard* me. He agreed: I had reached an impasse in my career. I needed to take the next step. In some way, or in all ways, Andrew helped engineer that.

I also know something more. As I sit in my apartment in San Francisco—one I share with Cambo, a fellow DK—taking in my own spectacular view of the city, and as I prepare for my debut on the Raiders pregame show, cohosting with former NFL coach Artie Gigantino, former NFL quarterback David Humm, and former hard-hitting Raiders legend George Atkinson, known with his partner in the defensive backfield, Jack Tatum, as the "criminal element," I know that Andrew feels flush with pride, as if I truly am his brother.

⌁

I enter the Black Hole.

I don't go in alone.

Raider Rob—black bandanna, black stocking cap, wraparound shades, dressed like a mix of a Black Panther and Darth Vader—escorts me in. The crowd in the Black Hole bellows.

Black Hole fanatics in bleacher seats high above wave, point, raise their fists in solidarity. I wave back. The fans in the Black Hole, many of them listeners, know who I am. They understand that in my heart I'm not a full-throttle Oakland Raiders fan—I bleed New York Giant blue and will never abandon my home team; I'm nothing if not loyal—but instead of condemning me, they accept me for it.

The Black Hole begins at the bottom of the south end zone and extends thirty rows up. Even before pregame warm-ups, the Black Hole is completely populated, filled with men, women, and a few of their children, decked out in some variation of Darth Vader, the Grim Reaper, a pirate, a black knight, a Hells Angel, a biker, a crypt keeper, a vampire, a deranged man or woman in black, and every possible combination thereof. The members of the Black Hole paint their faces in swirls, splotches, lines, or half in silver and half in black, or all in silver or all in black—expressive and frightening, postapocalyptic war paint. The Black Hole feels to me like a mosh pit gone wrong. The fans here approach every Raiders game as a fright fest and view every opposing player as fair game. The members of the Black Hole worship the Raiders. The team is their dark religion. They will drink their opponents' blood.

This day, Junior Seau, the great linebacker for the San Diego Chargers and one of the most intimidating players in the league, jogs onto the south end of the field to perform his pregame warm-up ritual. The members of the Black Hole see him bending and stretching in front of them, oblivious to them, and they go berserk. *They will not be ignored.* They rise to their feet, shake their fists, point, and then, as one, extend their middle fingers, thousands of middle fingers raised, and scream, "Fuck you, Seau!" and worse. Seau's concentration is obliterated and, annoyed, the intimidating linebacker moves to the other end of the field. The members of the Black Hole cheer and stomp as if the Raiders have scored a touchdown. I gape, stunned, reminding myself, *This isn't even the game. It's warm-ups.*

Before each pregame show, I spend some time in the Black Hole. I interview the fanatical fans, laugh with them, and eventually bond with them. I become an honorary member of the Black Hole. Years later, the members will induct me into the Black Hole Hall of Fame. Yes, there is such a thing. It is not in Canton, Ohio. You can find it online, but mostly it exists in a particular dark state of the imagination.

At the same time the Raiders hire me, the team brings in a new coach, the youngest in the league, blond, intense, charismatic Jon Gruden, who's only a couple years older than I am. I introduce myself before the first game, and Coach Gruden, nicknamed Chucky because of a resemblance to the murderous doll of the same name in the horror film *Child's Play*, greets me as if we've been friends for years.

"How you doing, JT? Good to see you. We're going to the top, man. You and me. Couple of rookies going to the *top*."

"I'm with you, Coach," I say, laughing. We form an instant relationship, fluid, fun, and easy, which is very helpful since, as part of the pregame show, I include a weekly coach's segment that I pretape in studio whenever the coach, known as a legendary workaholic, can break away from practice or game preparation. I occasionally wait two hours to tape his seven-minute interview. I don't care. Coach Gruden spews opinions and insights that crush the usual cliché-ridden canned vanilla blather you hear from coaches on the radio.

"Sorry to keep you waiting, JT," Coach Gruden says routinely before our interview segments.

"No worries, Coach."

"All right, let's do this. You ready?"

"I'm pumped."

And I am. After each segment I'm tempted to tell him that if this coaching gig doesn't work out, he should consider a future in broadcasting.

—

Following each pregame show, I head down to the field for the game and hang out in the Black Hole, sometimes making my way into the stands among the silver and black face-painted, costumed crazies and watching a quarter, screaming my lungs out with the best of them. In the second quarter, I walk along the sidelines, absorbing as many nuances of the game as I can. I want to be as close to the action as possible so I can bring that feeling to my listeners. I try to give the fan's perspective, but a fan with the best seat in the house, a guy with sideline access.

I notice that after the first couple of games, I've caught the attention of Bruce Allen. One day before a game, he seeks me out, and we walk the perimeter of the field together and talk about our mutual friend, Andrew.

"You talk to Bubba, JT? How's he doing?"

"I talked to him this morning. Right before I came to the stadium. He's great."

"He's the best. Tell him I say hello."

"I will."

And when I speak to Andrew, he often brings up Bruce. "Hey, how's GBA?"

"Who?"

"GBA. Gerald Bruce Allen."

I laugh. "Oh. He's great. He says hello."

"Say hi back. The guy's tremendous. I knew you two would hit it off."

I know Andrew. He's clearly happy that I've landed in San Francisco and that I'm hosting the Raiders pregame and postgame shows, but he's thrilled that he has connected me and Bruce. He loves championing my career; he *lives* for connecting his friends.

Before the third game of the season, after I finish the pregame show, I make my way to the sideline and watch the Raiders and their opponent of the day go through passing and kicking drills. I shade my eyes from the glint of the September afternoon sun. The shadow of Bruce Allen fills up the ten-yard space between us. He reaches me and we shake hands. "How'd the show go?"

"Real good. Lot of energy. Some great back-and-forth. We're really starting to find a groove."

"Excellent. Okay. It's time to meet Al."

Bruce starts to head across the field toward the 50-yard line.

I freeze.

Bruce whips around and faces me. "Come on. He wants to meet you."

Al Davis, owner of the Oakland Raiders and de facto general manager who makes every team decision short of calling plays, is described as a visionary, rebel, genius, and bully—among other names—and is considered the godfather of the NFL. He is without question the most controversial figure in all of football, running neck and neck with George Steinbrenner as the most controversial figure in all of sports, and he wants to meet *me*?

I can't move.

I've never felt intimidated by anyone in sports. Until now.

"JT," Bruce says. "Come on."

"Yeah, coming, sorry." I somehow will my legs to thaw and come alive. I take a step, then another, and then I catch up to Bruce. "He just, you know, has a reputation—"

"Definitely."

"I mean, he knows who I am?"

Bruce squints into the sun. "He knows everybody, JT."

I start to say something, but the words jumble and I clam up. I feel sweat leaking into my palms. Bruce must sense how nervous I am because he says, "There's nothing to worry about. Just don't say anything stupid."

We arrive at a phalanx of beefy security guards each the size of a lineman, one of whom nods at Bruce, eyes me, and steps aside, allowing us to approach Al Davis, who wears sunglasses and a Raiders sweat suit. He stands astride the fifty, hands clasped behind his back, scowling at the opposing team. He looks like a general assessing the enemy before a battle.

Bruce and I step closer. Al looks in our direction.

"Al, excuse me," Bruce says. "This is JT, our new pregame host."

Al lowers his head and peers at me over his sunglasses, keeping his hands locked behind him. "Hello, JT."

"Hello, Mr. Davis."

"Welcome. I'm looking forward to hearing what you can do this season. Good to have you."

"Thank you, sir."

Al turns away and continues his study of the opposing team. Meeting adjourned.

Fifteen seconds, most.

Bruce nods at me. We start walking back toward the sideline. This time I match him stride for stride.

"How did that go?" I say.

"Oh, great meeting," Bruce says. "He loves you."

———

Within weeks, my workload redlines, becoming almost too insane even for me. In addition to my night show, my hour-and-a-half Raiders pregame show, and my hour-and-a-half Raiders postgame show, I begin a midday show, five days a week, noon to three, without a cohost—solo, just me. I'm now on the air, live, eight hours every weekday, and three hours every Sunday. How do I do it? I'm fueled by coffee, my natural storehouse of energy, the need for only four hours of sleep a night, my ambition—my drive to become the best at what I do—and my focus on making as much money as possible. It's true. Alone in San Francisco, I keep going because I want to dominate as a sports talk host and I want to get rich.

I keep grounded by staying connected to my close friends, speaking often with my dad, and confiding my fears, triumphs, and complaints several times a day to Andrew. And Julie.

Despite the distance between us, we have no lull. We keep connected by phone and she flies up from Vegas on weekends. If anything, our relationship heats up, reaching a whole new level. I talk to Andrew about her. I tell him that I have no doubt: she is the one.

"Bring her down," he says. "Gotta meet her."

———

December 12, 1998.

I lie to Julie.

I tell her that we have a Saturday night work function, a fancy dinner at the Top of the Mark, the famous restaurant in the Mark Hopkins Hotel that overlooks the city, and that the two of us need to dress to impress.

Wasted from weeks of nonstop teaching, eyeing the finish line that looms ahead in just two weeks, allowing her the much-needed Christmas holiday and a solid week of rest, Julie arrives at my apartment in San Francisco just wanting to chill. "Do we really have to go to this work thing?" she says.

"Oh, yeah. Absolutely. It's a big deal."

"Who's gonna be there?"

"Oh, you know, my boss. And a couple of affiliates. Big. Very important."

"Is Andrew coming?"

"No. He can't make it."

She eyes me curiously. "I wish we could blow it off."

"No. Not possible. Done deal. Hey, look at the time. You better get dressed."

"We've got four hours."

I check my watch, laugh, and pull her in for a hug, looking past her through the window, quickly going through a mental checklist, making sure I've remembered everything. I know myself. With my schedule, I can get distracted or overtired and forget an important detail, like where I've left my keys. That cannot happen tonight.

At one point, I'm pretty sure Julie knows something is up. I hustle her out of the apartment and down the winding staircase to the lobby. She's dressed to kill and I'm wearing a suit. I shove my hand into my suit jacket pocket, feel for the small velvet box, make sure it's there, pull my hand out, and then five seconds later stick my hand back in and touch the box once more for reassurance.

Julie looks at me. She's seen every move. "Are you all right?"

"Me? Yeah. Perfect. You look great, by the way. Amazing."

"You, too. You clean up nice."

"This old thing? This suit's like ten years old. I wear it every night to do my show."

I try a laugh. She looks at me strangely. We hit the lobby and head outside into the cool December night. A stretch limousine waits at the curb. Seeing us, the driver, decked out in a black suit and driver's cap, springs out of the car and opens the back door for us.

"What's this?" Julie says.

"Our ride," I say. "The network sent it."

Her eyes narrow in suspicion but she doesn't say anything. We scramble into the backseat. A bottle of champagne chilling in an ice bucket faces us. I reach for it, prepare to pop the cork. "Champagne? Take the edge off?"

"Sure. Why not?"

She's on to me, I think. *She has to be. She's too smart.* And when the limo driver pulls over and parks facing the Golden Gate Bridge so we can sip champagne and take in the magnificent San Francisco skyline lit up by grids of twinkling lights, I'm sure she knows. Still, she says nothing. I do notice that as she takes a sip from her champagne flute, she goes strangely silent.

A couple hours later, as we finish our dinner at the Top of the Mark and my boss has yet to appear and the affiliates are no-shows, I'm positive she's figured it out. Of course it no longer matters, because even if she knows what's about to happen, we both know the pressure's on me.

I make my move right after the busboy clears away our dinner plates and our white-jacketed waiter dusts away the leftover crumbs with a golden crumb brush. I whistle out a slow, shallow breath, dig into my pocket for the thirtieth time—yep, it's still there—cup the small box in my hand, push my chair away, and in the middle of the Top of the Mark restaurant, as I have planned and imagined, I get down on one knee. I reach up, grab Julie's hand, and look up at her, focusing all of my love, my entire *life*, into the glow coming from her eyes.

"Julie," I say. "Will you—"

"Care for dessert?" The white-jacketed waiter stands above me, fondling a leather menu. "Our most famous, our signature, *les pommes au four*—"

"Dude," I say from my kneeling position. "Really? Do you see me down here? I'm *proposing*."

"Yes," Julie says.

"Wonderful," the waiter says. "Shall I bring two spoons?"

"I hope you were talking to me," I say to Julie.

She laughs, leans down, and we kiss.

I think the people sitting around us applaud, but that may be in my head. I'm too dazed and lost in the moment to be sure. Later, in the hotel suite at the Mark Hopkins that I booked earlier in the week and filled with flowers that afternoon, we call our parents and tell them the news. Julie's mind has already clicked into high-efficiency planning mode. We're looking at getting married in early September so she can finish the school year and take the summer to get everything together. We're planning a traditional church wedding, with a touch of Vegas. I already see us having the rehearsal dinner at the Hard Rock, and I want Andrew to speak.

———

We call it the Memorial Day Miracle.

May 31, 1999.

San Antonio, Texas.

Game two of the NBA Western Conference Finals between the Spurs and the Portland Trailblazers.

I watch Andrew work and I am in awe.

His energy, his size—his *presence*—fill up the room.

Even when the room is the Alamodome, a great barn of an arena where 40,000 raging, roaring fans work themselves into a frenzy, shaking the foundation of the building as the hometown Spurs overcome a seventeen-point deficit in the fourth quarter to pull within two points of Portland, 85–83, with nine seconds left in the game.

I, too, am caught up in the mayhem, standing courtside between Andrew and Julie. We have come at his invitation, the first time he and Julie have met. Friday, he picked us up at the airport, hugged us both, shouted, "This visit's long overdue!" then chauffeured us to his house, settled us into the guest room, and began blending a pitcher of margaritas. Since then, the margaritas have not stopped flowing.

The Spurs call a time-out and huddle just to the side of us. Andrew flips open his cell phone and becomes a fugue in motion, bending, pacing, shoving a hand through his mane of blond hair, gesturing like a frantic third base coach, his fingers slicing, dicing, and whirling in the air. Cradling the phone between chin and shoulder, he herds Julie and me down the sideline toward the tunnel at the corner of the arena that leads into the Spurs' dressing room.

The Spurs break their huddle, clap their hands in unison, and take the court, led by their "Twin Towers," David Robinson and Tim Duncan, and their sharpshooting small forward, Sean Elliott.

"This is *it*," Andrew shouts, his shrill, frantic voice piercing the din that envelops us. He closes the phone and cups it in his palm.

"Do or die," I shout back.

"Gonna win," he says. "*Gotta* win!"

His whole body nods, nearly in a genuflection. He beams, confident, any glimmer of doubt gone. He rolls back on his heels, bends his knees, claps his hands violently, and shouts something at the players, his grin wider.

A few feet in front of us, play starts. The ball finds its way into Sean Elliott's hands, and within moments, practically falling out of bounds, he launches a three-point shot that arcs seemingly forever in superslow motion before it nestles into the net with a soft *swish* that sings like a lullaby in all 80,000 of our ears.

The arena erupts in a vocal volcano and I shout and Julie screams and Andrew's face turns red, and although the game is not yet over, he sprints toward his broadcast crew, waving maniacally, a crazed orchestra conductor. When the game ends a minute later and the Spurs win 86–85 on Sean Elliott's miracle shot, Andrew corrals Elliott and the Spurs' point guard, the colorful Avery Johnson, he of the surprisingly high-pitched voice, for postgame interviews while Julie and I hug the wall of the tunnel, watching fans leaning over the railing, high-fiving Duncan and Robinson on their way past us. I crane my neck back toward the sideline and Andrew, cell phone slapped against his ear, lining someone up to his left, his fingers flying around in a circle, *works*, this arena his world, sports and radio his life.

Later, the three of us, strolling along River Walk, decompressing, wandering into a bar where people stand shoulder to shoulder and end to end, and cocktails magically slap into our hands, Andrew shouts, "What a fucking game!"

The patrons of the bar roar and then toast and drink with him.

"That was something to see," I say, not sure myself if I'm referring to the game or Andrew running the show on the sidelines.

"Damn, I love my *life*," he roars, pistol-shooting his pointer finger at the bartender for another round.

"So? Julie?" I say, stage-whispering into his ear. "What do you think?"

"Home run, babe. Grand slam."

I beam, tighten my grip on her hand. She presses back, leans over, and whispers into my other ear, "I love Andrew. He's such a teddy bear."

—

We hold the wedding rehearsal dinner for our closest friends and family in one of the Hard Rock's ballrooms. A month before I call Andrew and ask him to lead us off. "I want you to break the ice," I tell him.

"Yeah, babe," he says. "My honor."

Fourteen years later, reaching through the fuzz of memory, blurred by bottomless glasses of champagne and a flood of emotion, I remember the heart and sentiment of what Andrew says but not the exact words. He stands at his seat, clinks his glass with a spoon, and asks for attention. His size and presence fill the room and the eighty or so guests go quiet instantly. He looks at me and Julie and beams like a little kid with a great new toy. He places his hand over his heart. "I want to tell you about this couple," he says.

That's all it takes for me to tear up.

Julie grips my hand and squeezes.

"I think you all know why we're here at the Hard Rock," Andrew says, and with his hands animated, flying, stabbing the air, waving, he tells the story of how Julie and I met at the Rolling Stones concert. He talks about fate and he talks about connecting. He makes the audience laugh and he touches them. Finally, he raises his glass for a toast, and after we drink and he thanks everyone for listening, he receives a thunderous ovation.

After Andrew sits down, an undercurrent of people asking, "Who is he?" buzzes through the ballroom. He will soon answer the question himself. After Julie speaks and I say a few words, Andrew circulates, working the room, introducing himself to every person he doesn't know, flirting with my aunts, engaging my uncles, wowing my cousins. He holds court the way that only he can. By the end of the night, everybody knows—and loves—Andrew.

My life feels like a bullet train. After our wedding, we spend our honeymoon in Hawaii, the last week of relaxation and doing nothing that I can foresee. Realizing this, I'm antsy. Returning to San Francisco, I jump back into my hellacious two-shift days, shocking myself by staying energized and focused. I kick ass on the radio although I often emerge from the studio at two a.m. not sure what day it is or where I've parked my car. In late September, Jimmy Baxter calls to say that he's taken a job in telecommunications in San Francisco. While Julie prepares to relocate from Las Vegas, Jimmy and I spend hours each day apartment hunting for both of us. Finally we find apartments in the same complex. Jimmy, confirmed bachelor, grabs the stunning and expensive two-bedroom penthouse, while I, newly married and on a budget, rent a cramped yet affordable one-bedroom. *Welcome to married life*, I laugh to myself. The building is close to Jimmy's work and in the shadows of Pac Bell Park, the new baseball stadium under construction, a right fielder's throw from the studio, sticking to my cardinal rule: Never live more than five minutes from work.

In October, Julie arrives with all her possessions, including her baby, Luvie, a Maltese she acquired three weeks before we met. As Julie settles in, she offhandedly asks, "You checked with the landlord, right? This place takes dogs."

The look that sags across my face answers for her. "You didn't check," she says.

"I didn't. I will."

I do.

They don't.

Fortunately, Luvie weighs about five pounds, so whenever we feel the heat that the landlord will bust us or worry that an unfriendly neighbor will blow the whistle, we stash Luvie in my messenger bag, Julie's purse, or in a closet.

Shortly after Julie moves in, she hits me with big news.

She's pregnant.

I'm shocked. And then, instantly, I'm so happy I could scream. Clearly, we did *something* in Hawaii during those days of doing nothing.

I go to work a new man. It seems crazy but I feel full of *life*. Even though I'm brutalized by my eight hours on the radio, when I stagger home after my night show, go upstairs, and sneak Luvie out for her two fifteen a.m. walk, I suddenly consider myself an adult. More than that, I identify with my dad. I will soon be a member of his club, the dad society, living a life of worry and frustration, which is how I now know he lived day-to-day dealing with me. I'm sure he still feels that way. I haven't exactly chosen the most stable profession. The more I picture myself as a father, the more I realize that this is not only the role I've always wanted, it's the one I was meant to play.

Sometime before Christmas, Julie and I go to her doctor for a routine pregnancy appointment. The doctor spends a long time examining her, using the latest technology available. At one point, while Julie's still in her gown on the examining table, the doctor sits on a stool, wheels herself over to Julie, and takes Julie's hand. She has bad news. Julie has an ectopic pregnancy. The embryo has been implanted outside of the uterine cavity, in one of the Fallopian tubes. As I understand it, the embryo is not where it's supposed to be and Julie is going to have to terminate the pregnancy. The doctor gives Julie a shot of a powerful drug and predicts that Julie will have heavy bleeding. She assures us that we can try again after Julie's next cycle. The doctor sees how stricken I look, reaches over with her other hand, and squeezes my forearm. "I'm sorry," she says.

I sleepwalk through the rest of December as we gear up to enter the year 2000, the millennium year, known as Y2K. The world is on high alert. Many so-called experts, some of them alarmists, appear all over the media. They say that because of glitches in many of our computer systems, the moment the calendar flips from 1999 to 2000 an infection of digital bugs will invade every computer in existence, from our personal computers to computers that run businesses, banks, the government, and the military, essentially bringing the world to a stop and causing widespread panic and chaos.

As we approach New Year's Eve and Julie recovers from her

ectopic pregnancy, I feel as if the world has already stopped. We entertain friends on New Year's Eve and toast in the new century, all of us gulping champagne and swallowing liberal doses of doom, unwarranted, of course, as Y2K turns out to be a non-event.

A couple nights later, a Tuesday around eleven o'clock as I finish a segment with a caller and go to a break, the studio door opens and my producer leads in Julie, a surprise since she rarely visits me when I'm on the air. I rush around the console, hug her, and find her a chair facing me. She takes off her coat, places it on the back of the chair, and, sighing heavily, sits down on the chair in front of me. The past week has been typically hectic. As usual, because of my crazy schedule, we've rarely seen each other, connecting through phone calls, voice mails, and messages scribbled on notepads left on the kitchen counter. I crave some alone time with her. She's probably feeling the same way and has come to sit with me for a segment or two just to escape, to reconnect, to feel close. She asks for some water. I fill a glass from a pitcher I keep at my elbow.

I point at the clock on the wall that faces me, slip on my headset, and go into my next segment. I deliver an outrageous take to try to get a rise out of my listeners and get the phone lines to light up. It works. I take a call from Benny Jet, one of my favorite callers, nod and smile at Julie.

She stares at me across the console. Her lips seem caked and cracked and her face looks ghost white. She lowers her head into her hands. All I can see now is the top of her head. I finish the call, take another, and squirm in my chair, wondering why Julie won't lift her head. Ten seconds pass, twenty, and still she keeps her head down, resting it in her hands. The call ends. The phone lines flash, full now, all eight lines pulsing red as the show heats up. I grab another call. Frustrated with the caller, I lose it, cut him off, and hear my own voice cracking, sounding like a stranger talking to me through my headset.

And still Julie's head is down.

A new caller says something. I answer back, stumble over my words, my eyes on the top of Julie's head. The caller calls me out, catches me in a contradiction.

Julie lifts her head.

Her forehead is a swamp.

She peers at me, trying to find me, her blue eyes gone glassy and vacant.

She opens her mouth to say something and then she pitches forward.

I hang up on the caller, shut down my sound, whip off my headset, shout, "Call 911!" and run to the other side of the console.

"Julie!"

"I'm—"

She's conscious but she can't speak.

I cradle her head in my arms. "Call an *ambulance*!" I yell into the empty room.

And then everything in my sight line shimmers and after an endless minute a figure bursts into the room, running, it seems, in slow motion. I can make out his voice and identify him, Lee Hammer, the program director at the station. He shouts, the words flowing out of his mouth. I blink and I see them in block letters in front of me—"Ambulance coming." In my arms Julie looks so pale, so very pale, and then two more figures hurry in, men in blue, and the next thing I know, as if I'm the one falling in and out of consciousness, we're riding in the back of an ambulance, the siren screaming, Julie strapped to a gurney. I sit beside her, holding her hand, and voices crackle through the tinny dispatch speakers up front, something about her blood pressure dropping, and a man in blue asks me, "Is there anything we need to know about? Does she take any regular medication? Does she have an ongoing condition?"

"She was pregnant," I say.

More crackling knifes through the speakers again, more insistent this time, and I hear the words "No! Go to UCSF!" I feel the ambulance whip around and change course. *We're going to the wrong place?* I think, fingers of panic gripping me by the throat, and I hover over Julie, so pale, so distant, and I somehow know that every second matters.

The ambulance roars up a ramp and jerks to a stop. Its back doors fly open and I roll out, dazed, my breathing coming fast, and then the two men in blue slide Julie out of the ambulance on the gurney. They break into a run and push her through the doors of the ER. I follow alongside, trying to keep up, muttering some ridiculous words of reassurance. "I'm right here," "It's okay," "You're gonna be fine." It all sounds hollow and canned, but I repeat every word to myself over and over in what I realize is the first of what will be a hundred prayers.

More words and phrases tumble around me. "Relationship to the admitted," "Paperwork," "Insurance information." But I can't find the strength to answer and I won't leave Julie's side. And then we crash through another set of double doors and enter a kind of lobby that makes me feel as if we made a wrong turn into a Holiday Inn. Then the gurney turns down a corridor with scuffed, slick floors. We veer left, everyone on the run, the squeaking of the gurney's wheels on the floor a pinging backbeat to our huffing breaths, and then, *wham*, we slam through a final set of doors. People in green smocks and surgical masks flock around us, shove their way between Julie and me. One of them pulls off Julie's rings—her brand-new wedding band and her diamond engagement ring that I financed and my parents bought in the diamond district in Manhattan and I presented to Julie on my knees at the Top of the Mark in San Francisco—and a doctor in a green smock, his surgical mask worn around his neck like a lanyard he made at summer camp, hands me Julie's jewelry and says, "I'll do the best I can."

A wall of green blocks me from Julie and the gurney as another person in a green smock wheels her away through yet another set of double doors. Helplessly, I watch her disappear, her rings suddenly feeling sharp and cold in my hands. I close my fingers around her jewelry and make a fist, and I stop a green-smocked woman moving quickly toward this last set of doors and say, my eyes filling up, "What's going on? Do you know what's going on with my wife?"

"Hemorrhage in her Fallopian tube," she says. "Everything points to that."

I know enough to understand then what has happened. I unfold my fist and glance at Julie's rings, and the green-smocked woman guides me to a hallway with an opening in the middle that looks like a bank teller's window.

I complete the necessary paperwork, find a pay phone, and

dial Jimmy Baxter's number. I don't need to tell him much. *Emergency room, Julie, UCSF Hospital, I don't know.* That's all I can say and all he needs to hear. He's on his way.

When Jimmy arrives, we stake out a section in the corner of the waiting room and prepare for an all-nighter. We don't talk much. I can't sit still. I pace the waiting room, go out into the hall, press my back against the wall, and I pray. "Please let Julie be all right," I say quietly. "Please."

Finally, after an hour or more, a young doctor comes into the waiting room wearing paper over his shoes that crinkles as he walks toward me. I stand and he leads me to the far side of the waiting room. His face looks creased and gray even though he can't be more than thirty.

"Your wife's out of danger," he says.

I want to hug him or at least pump his hand, but all I can manage to say is, "Thank you, Doctor." Then I repeat, "Thank you."

"It was a little touch and go. One of her Fallopian tubes ruptured."

I blink rapidly. "Okay," I say.

"We had to remove the tube."

"By rupture—"

"Picture a hand grenade rolling into a narrow tube and then, boom, it explodes."

This guy has played a lot of video games, I think.

"Will she . . . will we—"

"Yes, she'll still be able to conceive." The doctor rests his hand on my shoulder. "It shouldn't be too long before you can see her."

He smiles, turns toward the door, and, paper shoes crinkling, ducks out of the waiting room.

I walk back to Jimmy, who leans forward on the scratchy couch where we've camped out in the corner.

"What did he say?" Jimmy asks.

"She's gonna be all right."

Jimmy exhales and I sit down next to him and collapse into the couch.

I have to be strong, I tell myself, *for Julie, and for the family I know we will make together, someday.*

I lower my head into my hands, blinking furiously, batting back tears.

———

Julie's at home, on bed rest, her mom visiting, caring for her and saving me. Like a fullback hitting the line grinding out three yards at a time, I put my head down and drive forward, shouting eight hours of high-energy sports talk every day and into every night. According to her doctor, once Julie recovers completely from the surgery and her body resumes its normal cycle, she can try to get pregnant again.

I desperately want to try again. I know women have to be conscious of their biological clocks, but I, too, hear something ticking inside me, either my own biological clock or a time bomb ready to blow. Years later, when we talk about the days after her surgery, Julie will say that the loss of her Fallopian tube and the possibility that we couldn't have a family absolutely wrecked me, messed me up even more than it did her.

Two weeks after Julie's surgery, my body feels as if it's caving in on itself. I walk through life a zombie, emotionally and physically wasted. Sometimes I feel myself gasping for air as if I've just sprinted a hundred yards. Night after night, walking home after the show, feelings of deep and surprising loss rip into me. I don't tell Julie how I feel. When I'm with her, I'm steady as a rock, or at least I pretend to be. But when I'm alone, in the shower, or walking the dog, I unclench and release what I've been holding in, and the loss returns and shoots through me, darkening my heart. I wonder if Julie knows how deeply wounded I am. I believe she does. At certain moments, as she regains her strength, she searches my face with her eyes and nods slowly, her lips moving slightly. *I know how you feel, John*, she seems to say, and she drenches me with a sunny, sympathetic smile, insisting wordlessly that everything will be all right. I know she's faking it. I don't mind. I'm faking it, too.

One night after Julie's mom returns to Illinois, I end my show, head home, hit the lobby elevator at two ten a.m., and step into our apartment. Luvie greets me excitedly, her tiny tail wagging wildly. I slip the leash over her little neck, carry her into the elevator, and, her tiny body curled against my chest, ride down the nine floors to the lobby.

I step outside into the damp, cool night, place the Maltese in her spot fifty feet from the building, and wait for her to sniff around in the bushes and get comfortable. Luvie circles, lowers her butt, and prepares for her two a.m. drop. I look away—even dogs deserve privacy at such times—and I think about an ad I saw that day in one of the trade magazines announcing a new Fox radio network coming soon, based in Los Angeles, to be broadcast nationwide. I know I'm in some altered, dazed state, but I fixate on that ad. It feels like a message meant only for me. *I have to go there,* I say to myself. *I have to be on that network, as soon as possible. I have to get out of here.*

A wave of exhaustion hits me. Too tired to even lift the five-pound dog, I lead Luvie back into the building and press the button for the elevator. The elevator arrives. I enter, Luvie on her leash behind me. I press 9 and watch the elevator doors rumble and close—on Luvie's leash. The elevator jerks violently and rises and the leash snaps. I look down. Luvie is gone.

I scream and pound every number for every floor. The elevator bangs to a stop on four and I punch the button for the lobby with my fist. The elevator doors shimmy, hesitate.

"Come on! Come *on!*"

I slam my hand on the lobby button. Holding the remains of Luvie's leash, I dash out of the elevator and run into the stairwell. I race down the stairs, my heart pounding. I picture Luvie lying in a pool of blood on the white phony marble floor of the lobby. *What will I tell Julie? How will she ever be able to deal with this?* I feel like a murderer. I whirl around the corner, my feet nearly flying out from under me, maintain my balance by pressing my hand onto the floor, and I shout, "Luvie!" I turn into the lobby. Luvie faces the elevator, looking shaken and confused. She sees me and bolts toward me. I scoop her into my arms, carry her back into the elevator, and hold her close as we ride to the ninth floor and our apartment. We're both trembling.

"I thought I killed you," I say, burying my face in her fur.

Luvie whimpers.

I start to shiver.

In the hallway outside our door, I pat myself down in search of my key, find it, and, my hands trembling, locate the lock, insert the key, and push open the door to our apartment. I gently put Luvie down on the floor and stumble into the kitchen. I lower myself into a chair at the kitchen table, and, knowing that Luvie is safe, I bend over, exhale, and cry. Since the night at the hospital weeks ago, I've held myself together with adrenaline and caffeine, but now, in the dark, Luvie and I safe at home, I let it all out, my chest heaving with sobs.

I have never felt so alone.

———

I call Andrew and ask him about the new Fox radio network. He tells me the network has great pedigree. Tom Lee, who runs KJR in Seattle, a guy he knows well and a friend of mine, has been tapped to run the network. Plus Kraig Kitchin, the head of Premiere, the parent company, is one of the most respected people in all of radio. Andrew says I should definitely go there.

But not now.

"Why not?" I ask him. "Isn't it good to be in on the ground floor?"

"Not in radio," he says. "Here's what's gonna happen. Never fails. They'll set the lineup and within a few months or a year, they'll fire everybody. *Then* you go in."

"I gotta get out of here," I say. "I don't know how long I can last. The schedule is brutal. Plus, Julie…"

I let my voice trail off. I don't have to say anything. Andrew knows.

"I hear you." Andrew pauses. "You want to move to San Antonio? I'll find you a spot."

"Seriously?"

"Seriously."

"Wow. I don't know. I mean, that would be great, to work together. I just—"

"Think about it. Take your time. The offer stands."

"Thanks, man."

"Talk to you later."

I do consider Andrew's offer. I talk to Julie. We both want to leave San Francisco, but we face a slight stumbling block. I want to move to Los Angeles and she wants to move back to Las Vegas. I call Andrew later and tell him I want to talk to Lisa and Matt, my agents, and feel them out. I want to at least mention my interest in Fox. He agrees. I call them the next morning. I ask them what they think about trying to find a place for me on the new Fox network.

"You don't want to be in the first wave," Lisa says.

"They fire everybody," Matt says.

"Never fails," Lisa says.

"They all get the ax," Matt says.

"That would be a good place for you, though," Lisa says.

"But you don't want to go now," Matt says.

"Absolutely not," Lisa says. "We'll get you in the second wave. After they throw out the whole first lineup."

"Never fails," Matt says.

At the Super Bowl in Atlanta, Andrew and I spend the entire week hanging out, both on and off Radio Row. At night before my show I pop into the nonstop party he throws in his hotel suite, which seems to me the real nightly show, a running conversation with VIPs and on-air talent, accompanied by rivers of alcohol and enough food for twenty tailgate parties. As usual Andrew holds court as host, headliner, consummate storyteller, constant hugger, the larger-than-life main attraction. We stick tight to each other, roaming Radio Row, bonding with the bigwigs who run the nation's most powerful and important sports talk radio stations and networks. We've never been closer.

As the millennium year moves from winter into spring, we watch San Francisco puff out, a bubble threatening to burst. From the windows in our small, increasingly cramped ninth-floor apartment, we see new construction all around us, walling us in, the result of the dot-com boom. A Starbucks pops up on every corner, a hot new restaurant opens every month, each populated with brash twenty-one-year-old millionaires, their portfolios bulging with cash because they've recently sold their Pets.com and I-bids and now have nothing to do except peck away at their laptops and wallow in their wealth. At the end of the summer, a miracle happens.

Julie gets pregnant again.

"I don't want to give birth here," she says calmly, with unwavering conviction. "I want to go back to Vegas. I'm more comfortable there. It's also closer for my family. It's better for us."

"I hear you," I say, and I do. And while she doesn't connect her ectopic pregnancy to the city itself, in some way I do. And so we plot our escape.

As we ease into football season, I talk it over with Andrew.

"I'll just do my two shifts from Vegas, like before, and commute on the weekends for the Raiders. It wouldn't be that big a deal."

I can almost see him vigorously nodding his head. "I agree. Very doable."

"What do I tell my bosses? They might not like the idea."

"Maybe you don't tell them."

I pause and try this idea on. "Just leave," I say, finally.

"Yeah. Once you're up and running and everything's going smooth, then tell them. As long as you're doing your job, they won't care."

"Julie really doesn't want to be here," I say.

"Unhappy wife, unhappy life."

"Good line. Sums it all up nice. Where'd you hear that?"

"A rerun of *Married . . . with Children*," Andrew says.

"I'm gonna do it," I say.

———

We get out of our lease and set up movers. During Super Bowl week 2001, as the movers leave for Las Vegas and Andrew and I work Radio Row from Tampa before the game between the Baltimore Ravens and the New York Giants, the week the country inaugurates George W. Bush, Julie and her mom pack up our car and drive from San Francisco to Las Vegas with Luvie, stopping overnight in Bakersfield in a cheap motel to watch the inauguration. By the time I return from the Super Bowl, Julie has us moved in, our place set up as if we'd been living there for months.

I reunite with Bobby Machado in Vegas. In no time he has us up and running from the small studio just off the Las Vegas Strip, near Mandalay Bay. Maybe it's the thrill of ducking out of San Francisco like a couple of fugitives, but Bobby and I rock out in Vegas. Night after night before I rush home to check on my very pregnant wife and catch a few hours of sleep before I return for the daytime shift, Bobby and I agree that I'm doing the best work of my life.

Of course, I wonder when my bosses will figure out that I'm gone. I've got my story set. I'll tell them the truth. Well, mostly. I'll just say that Julie wanted to have the baby in Vegas, so we bolted. If they give me a hard time, I'll say, "I thought I told you I was gonna do the show from Vegas. I swear I told you."

I know, lame. But it's all I got.

In early March, I take a trip to San Antonio to hang with Andrew during the Spurs NBA play-off run. When I get back, Bobby pops in to see me before my night show. He looks troubled. "Something's going on," he says.

"Like what?"

"A couple guys at the network got canned over the weekend. Low-level execs."

"So what? It's radio."

"They're not being replaced."

Now, that is not good.

"Okay. Anything else?"

"Yeah. I'm hearing there's problems with the parent company in New York."

"What kind of problems?"

"Liquidity problems."

"Probably bullshit," I say.

"Unless—"

"Unless it's the truth," I say.

It's too much to say that my nose twitches and I smell it.

But I do sense it.

Trouble.

I feel for Bobby. If I'm right and he loses this job, he has nothing to fall back on. I'm covered. I recently signed a two-year contract extension. The ink's not even dry yet. Plus, I have agents who have my back. I promise myself that if I can do anything to protect Bobby, I will.

I check the time and start to barge into the studio. I turn back to Bobby, who looks comatose. "Hey, man, we'll worry for real when the checks stop coming."

The checks don't stop coming, but they slow down. My next paycheck arrives five days late.

The weeks pass, and every Friday I hear about somebody new getting the ax, being called into the boss's office and handed a severance package. I look over the programming schedule and determine that I am, by far, the highest-paid host at the network, especially since Sports Fan opted out of the Pete Rose business a while ago, shortly after I moved to San Francisco. My agents tell me not to worry, I have a contract.

I also have a baby on the way.

I worry.

The network starts making subtle cuts in programming, first laying off update guys. Then they grab a bigger knife and make more drastic cuts, dropping one show and filling the time slot by replaying my previous night's show. Soon they lop off my afternoon show and replace that with some cheap syndicated show. I get the word in early April that I will no longer have anybody doing sports updates. I'll have to do them myself. Now, whenever I go to a break, Bobby slides a sheet in front of me with the latest sports scores, which I read twenty minutes past and twenty minutes before every hour.

"Do they want me to read all the commercial spots, too?" I scream at Bobby. "What *bullshit*." I ball up the paper with the sports scores and pitch it against the wall.

By late April, I feel like the last man standing.

I call Andrew in a panic. "They owe me a shitload of money—my salary, plus over fifty grand in my IRA they've supposedly been funding."

"You're covered," Andrew says.

"Yeah, I know, I got Matt and Lisa."

"And you got me."

I exhale. "Thanks."

"Remember, worst comes to worst, you got a job here."

"I know. I appreciate that. But Julie, the baby. I mean, I love San Antonio—"

"Worst comes to worst," Andrew says.

"So, what do I do in the meantime?"

"Nothing. You do nothing. You stay put. You keep being the

good soldier. You can't quit. You let them fire you. It's the only way to protect yourself."

"Okay."

"I'll let you know if I hear anything. You do the same."

"Deal."

Two nights later, as I finish my twenty-to-one a.m. sports update and go to a commercial, behind the glass, facing me, Bobby suddenly bolts out of the control room and disappears. He returns moments later wheeling in a shopping cart. He pulls a screwdriver out of his hoodie pocket and starts unscrewing the cassette deck that's attached to the main console. I fly out of my seat and run over to him. Head down, a man on a mission, he frantically unscrews the last remaining screw, yanks the cassette deck out of the console, and places it into the shopping cart. He moves over to another piece of equipment, a zephyr, and starts detaching that.

"Bobby, what the fuck are you doing?"

"Covering my ass," he says. And then he stares at me as if I am without a clue. "It's over. You see that, right?"

"They haven't said so officially—"

"It's *over*. I'm taking anything that's not welded down."

"I'm not sure that's a great idea—"

Bobby doesn't hear me, or ignores me, or thinks I'm hopeless. He bends over the console and starts untangling a mass of wires so he can access the zephyr. The wires out of his way, he goes after the equipment with his screwdriver like a deranged electrician.

We barely speak for the remaining hour and ten minutes of the show. During commercial breaks, Bobby pulls everything out of the control room that he can. The show ends and Bobby leaves the control room, pushing the shopping cart, which is now loaded with electrical equipment.

Outside the Mandalay Bay, I walk to my car, catching a glimpse of Bobby in the distance, pushing the shopping cart filled with electronics toward his apartment building. The uncertainty of my future presses in on me. I feel as if the company has shot a bullet into my tomorrow.

—

The next day, I get the word from a guy I don't know.

First, he says, have Bobby bring back all the equipment by the end of the day and all will be forgiven, no harm, no foul. If he doesn't return all the stuff, they will bring charges. Grumbling, Bobby pushes the shopping cart back and returns everything, reluctantly.

As for me, I have no more contract and no IRA because the company has filed for bankruptcy.

The company has gone under and waited until the absolute last second to tell me.

I'm unemployed and I'm furious.

But mostly, I'm scared.

Andrew calls me hourly to calm me and reassure me. "It's gonna be all right. I swear. You caught a bad break. You're momentarily out of work. It's radio. Happened to me, happens to everybody."

"It's never happened to me," I say.

"You got the best people in the world working for you," Andrew says. "It's gonna be okay."

"Julie," I say. "We've having a baby in a few months. Where am I gonna work? There are no sports talk stations in Vegas."

"Trust me," Andrew says.

"Do you know something?"

"Not exactly."

"But you can read the room," I say.

He laughs. "Sometimes." And he adds, for emphasis, "Don't worry. *Trust* me, JT."

I do.

I trust Andrew with my life.

Within two weeks, I get a call from Matt and Lisa.

"You sitting down?" Lisa says.

"You should be," Matt says.

"Tom Lee," Lisa says.

"Fox Sports Radio in L.A.," Matt says.

"The second wave, remember?" Lisa says.

"They've made some big changes in their lineup," Lisa says.

"As we predicted," Matt says.

"You're all set. We got you Monday through Friday," Lisa says.

"Four to seven," Matt says.

"No overnights?" I say.

"*Days, four to seven*," Lisa says.

"And wait until you hear the money," Matt says.

"When do I start?" I ask.

"We're working on the exact date," Lisa says.

"The last detail," Matt says.

"After the baby's born, right?"

"Yes. At least a couple weeks into July," Matt says.

"How am I gonna do this, with the baby?"

"You'll commute for a few weeks," Lisa says.

"You do that now, right?" Matt says.

"You'll move the wife and kid to L.A. at the end of the summer," Lisa says.

"L.A. I can think of a lot worse places," Matt says.

"Yeah," Lisa says, blowing out a laugh. "San Francisco."

"Yeah, right," Matt says, laughing along with her.

"They'll pay for your move, too," Lisa says.

"Wow," I say.

"I guarantee you this," Lisa says. "Clear Channel and Premiere, which owns Fox Sports Radio? They're not going out of business."

"Jim Rome, Dr. Laura, Rush. They'll be around for a while," Matt says.

"You'll have to fuck this one up all by yourself," Lisa says.

"But try not to," Matt says.

John Michael Tournour arrives May 24, 2001, six weeks early. The first time I see him, I gasp. He's tiny, five pounds or so, and looks beat up. The crown of his head is slightly pointy and his right arm is slack. He's so beautiful he takes my breath away.

"He looks a little banged up," I blurt to the nurse.

"Natural for preemies. He'll be fine."

"My son," I say squatting down next to Julie in the hospital room, holding her hand, my eyes riveted on the baby. "We have a son."

"He must be special," Julie says, "because today is a special day."

It hits me only then.

Today—May 24—is my dad's birthday.

After Julie and Johnny conk out, I find a phone and call my dad, who is spending the day with his sister and brother back in New York.

"Dad," I say, and I start to choke. I can hardly speak. I take a deep breath and the words come out haltingly, "I wanted to tell you...you've got a grandson. He was born today...we're naming him after you. John Michael."

I think my dad says something.

I can't tell for sure because I lose it. My chest heaves with sobs and tears flood my cheeks.

Dad, I say to myself because the words remain in my throat, muffled with my sobs, words that I know I could never say aloud. *I have spent my life trying to make you proud. I didn't know how to do it. Until now. I thought making you proud meant having a great career and making a lot of money. It's not. It's about this moment, having a family. Being a dad. It's about your grandson.*

On the other end of the phone, I hear another sound. I wait a moment and the sound becomes gradually clearer until I can finally make it out...

My dad quietly crying.

I see in front of me as if in a photo album the three generations of fathers and sons, all of us bearing the same name.

Father, Son, Grandson.

My handoff.

10.

The Boss of Me

Los Angeles
2001–2004

ON A BRIGHT late summer afternoon in July, I turn off the 405 Freeway onto Sunset Boulevard, weave my way past UCLA and through Beverly Hills, whiz by the historic Beverly Hills Hotel, Tudor-style movie star mansions, Sunset Strip landmarks such as the Roxy, Whisky a Go Go, and Tower Records, then turn left at Sunset Plaza and drive up into the Hollywood Hills. The road winds through a canyon past thickets of palm trees, designer homes on stilts, and a second wave of movie star mansions hidden behind ornate metal gates and built into the side of the mountain. I pop in my second Rush CD of the trip, find "New World Man," and crank it up. I howl along to the lyrics because that's how I feel, like a freaking new world man. I live in L.A. Well, Sherman Oaks in the San Fernando Valley to be exact, but close enough, and my choice because my house sits less than a mile from the studio, of course. I have a new baby, Jason, born one month ago, June 18, 2003, arriving in a hurry and without a hitch, our second son, taking my breath away and stealing my heart, second time in two years. Johnny, the older brother now, is two, a handful, a little jock in the making, a miniature me, I fear. As for work, I've re-upped, Lisa and Matt forging a sweet multiyear deal. I work with a strong producer who runs the board and watches my back, and the way I hear it, my talk show rocks. I feel it, too. I know I'm doing my best radio ever. I own my time slot, and maybe I can't help it, or maybe it's the way I feel, but I walk into work early every evening with a swagger, a gunslinger about to blow you away, the boy from New York City taking L.A. and the nation at night by storm. I have to say, I've come a long way from cold-calling stocks. And now add *this* to the mix, the reason I'm tooling up into the Hollywood Hills on a midsummer afternoon. Not everybody gets this privilege. Life, as Andrew always says, is grand.

I turn the music up, blast it so loud the car roof vibrates, and then check the clock on the dashboard to make sure I'm not late. I'm good. In fact, I'm running a few minutes early. I slow down, and as I twist my way toward Mulholland Drive I catch a glimpse of this crazy quilt of a city stretched out on either side of this hill, L.A. behind me, the Valley in front, an endless patchwork of squares housing ten million people, rolling out toward the horizon. I glance at the clock again. Still fine. I tap my thumbs on the steering wheel, find the drumbeat along with Neil Peart. No, I'm not nervous. I just don't want to be late for Jim Brown.

Yes, *the* Jim Brown, former NFL great, to my mind the best player ever to play the game. Hollywood movie star and action hero of *The Dirty Dozen* and many other box office hits, civil rights activist, founder of Amer-I-Can, an organization dedicated to stopping gang violence in our cities, he's the only guest I pay to come on my show. When I was settling in at Fox two years ago, my boss presented me with a budget for guests consisting of $750 a week, a pittance. He said I could distribute the money any way I wanted, among as many guests as I could, as long as I didn't go over the seven fifty. I bitched to Julie and of course to Andrew, and then it hit me. I knew how to allocate the money. I had done a couple of segments with Jim Brown and we had really connected. He was much more than a former jock. He was a difference maker, someone who'd gone through a lot, made mistakes, owned them, and now wanted to give back in a big way. Jim brought a perspective and an insight to football and to life that I wanted to tap into every week. He offered something you couldn't hear on any other show. Plus, we did damn good radio. Forget about booking anyone else. I could power through my show without any other guests, leading off each hour with my intense, high energy, unstoppable monologue, and then spending the rest of the show bantering with my callers, the best in the business.

I invited Jim to appear with me every week by phone, offering him my entire budget. When Jim heard the number, he laughed.

"That's all I got for guests," I said. "I'm giving you my entire budget."

Jim laughed again and then accepted my offer. Now, after one kick-ass season working together, the network has offered him a contract for the following year.

Amazing, since Jim and I have never met in person.

"You gotta sign the contract," I say to him off the air, on the phone, before our last segment.

"Come on up to the house next week, JT," Jim said. "Bring the contract and I'll sign it."

Now, slowing as I reach the crest of the hill, almost to Mulholland Drive, I check the street address that I scribbled on the sheet of paper splayed on the passenger seat and pull into the long driveway of a wide ranch-style house. I park behind a shiny black Range Rover tricked out with green-tinted windows and gleaming mag wheels, the last in a line of a half-dozen brand-new SUVs filling up the entire length of the driveway. I grab a manila folder containing the contracts, jump down from my own SUV, rust-colored, *the* suburban couple staff car, cluttered with newborn and kid paraphernalia—car seat, empty crushed apple juice boxes, blankets, rattles, squeaky toys, and one battered pacifier—and make my way to Jim Brown's front door. As I pass the line of Range Rovers, Land Rovers, and Escalades, I decide that Jim is entertaining a sports celebrity and his entourage. Not a surprise. He often invites NFL players to his home, most recently running back Curtis Martin, whose game and character he respects.

I hesitate, slap the manila folder against my thigh, and knock on the front door. After a few seconds, I hear footsteps, and a bodyguard the size of a nose tackle opens the door.

"JT," I say. "I'm here to see Jim. He's expecting me."

"I know," the bodyguard says.

He stands aside, motions me in, but his girth allows me barely enough room to squeeze by.

I walk into Jim's house and see before me and on all sides a panoramic view of the city through walls of glass windows. As I step inside I feel as if I'm walking on a cloud looking down at the city.

"Follow me," the bodyguard says.

Another few steps and we enter the living room, where twenty young men dressed in jeans and T-shirts or tank tops, looking out of place and dangerous, cluster around Jim Brown, who sits on a straight-backed chair in the center of the room, as if he is a judge, a mediator, or a college professor holding a class at his home. I know at once that the young men who surround Jim belong to gangs in the city, perhaps Crips and Bloods. Some sit on chairs on either side of Jim, others hang back, huddled together. The tension in the room crackles. I have felt similar tension—so hot it burns the air around you—only twice in my life: in college before a fight when I was a DK and we fought the Brockport rugby team when they invaded our campus, and at the MGM Grand Hotel the night of the Holyfield-Tyson fight.

One of the gang members leans forward in his chair and says something to Jim. He speaks softly, just about a whisper. I strain to hear.

"It's about territory..."

Jim, shaking his head slowly, answers just as quietly, "The violence, the killing, it has to stop."

I tuck myself into a corner to wait it out, but Jim sees me in his periphery and, without moving a muscle, says, "Hi, JT."

I feel every head turn toward me. I smile like an idiot, raise the manila folder and hold it up in the air, and say, "Hi, Jim. If this is a bad time—"

"Just drop those documents on the table," Jim says. "I'll sign them later."

"Perfect," I say.

Feeling as if a spotlight has clicked on above me, I step forward and place the folder on a coffee table a few feet away, turn, and start to ease out of the room.

"I appreciate you coming up here, JT," Jim says. "We'll spend more time together next time."

"Beautiful," I say.

I couldn't sound lamer. I want to disappear, or at least sprint the hell out of there, but head high, slipping past a couple of possible Crips who stare down a couple of possible Bloods, I walk out of the room, escorted once again by the bodyguard who I realize is not there to protect Jim but to protect *me*.

———

A few weeks later, before our segment together, Jim and I spend some time catching up.

"Raiders playing Cleveland next week," Jim says. "I'm going up to Oakland for the game."

"Any chance I can put you on the pregame show?"

"Sounds good," Jim says, and then whistles softly. "Al Davis. Amazing man."

"Oh, yeah. One of a kind. When's the last time you saw him?"

Jim hesitates. "I don't know. It's got to be fifteen years."

"Wow. Really?" An idea clicks into place. "Would you like me to set up a meeting with the two of you?"

"I'd love to see Mr. Davis. It's been too long."

THE BOSS OF ME

"Done," I say. "I'll make it happen."

The producer waves a finger in my face and Jim and I go into our segment. Afterward, everyone in the vicinity compliments me on another hot seven minutes of radio with Jim Brown, but all I can hear is the sound of my own voice slamming one word back at me inside my skull: *"DONE."*

And then I say aloud, "I better make this happen."

—

I call Fudgie, Al Davis's longtime secretary and, speaking hurriedly to mask the anxiety I feel, tell her that Jim Brown would like to sit down with Mr. Davis. I ask if there is any way I can set that up.

"I'll have to call you back," Fudgie says.

Terrific. If she doesn't come through, I'll lose all credibility with Jim Brown. I'm gonna look like a jerk.

I call Andrew to calm me down.

"What if she doesn't make it happen, bro?" I say to him. "You'll have to talk me down off the ledge."

He laughs.

"It's not funny," I say.

"Oh, babe, I'm picturing you tap-dancing your ass off, trying to explain to the toughest football player who ever lived why Al Davis won't see him."

"Not funny at all," I say.

Andrew laughs harder.

Fudgie calls me a few days later. She tells me to bring Jim Brown up to Mr. Davis's box before the game.

"Thank *you*," I say, trying not to appear overly giddy with relief.

Three hours before the Oakland-Cleveland game I walk onto the field and wave to a stadium attendant. He disappears into a tunnel and returns a moment later driving a golf cart. He pulls the cart over to me and I step in. I search the field and see Jim Brown sitting alone on the Raiders bench reading a newspaper. The stadium feels eerily empty, the only sound coming from two players grunting, kicking up the turf as they run pass patterns. The attendant drives the golf cart over to Jim and parks behind the bench. I step out and walk up to him.

"Hey, Jim," I say.

Jim folds up the newspaper and squints at me. "JT, how are you?"

"I'm good. So, you ready to see Mr. Davis?"

"Let's do it."

Jim stands up and begins walking slowly, painfully, toward the golf cart. He eases himself in and then nods almost imperceptibly, my signal that we're good to go. The attendant drives to the far end of the stadium, to the elevators, and parks the golf cart. As Jim pulls himself out of the cart, I swing around and press the button for the elevator. Jim walks slowly over to the elevators and leans against the stadium wall. The elevator arrives and we head inside, Jim grimacing with every step he takes. He shakes his head and I press the button that will take us to the top floor, to Al Davis's suite. In nine seasons as a record-breaking running back in the NFL, Jim lived by the philosophy, "When someone tackles you, make sure he feels it worse than you," but all those years and all those hits have left him with ruined knees.

The elevator doors open and Jim and I walk out. Another golf cart, with another stadium attendant at the wheel, sits five feet away. Without a word, Jim lowers himself into the passenger seat. The driver takes us the length of the walkway to Mr. Davis's owner's suite. Again, I rush out while Jim pulls himself out of the golf cart. I knock on the door, which is slightly ajar. Al Davis murmurs, "Come in."

I walk in and see Al Davis sitting at his desk. "Hello, JT," he says.

"Mr. Davis, hello. Jim Brown's here to see you."

Al gets up from his desk and moves toward me just as Jim enters the room. The two men stop and face each other across the room. I look from one man to the other and see them each break into a smile at the same time.

"There he is," Al Davis says. "Look at him. Jim Brown."

Jim chuckles. "Hello, Mr. Davis."

Al Davis crosses the room in a couple of strides, reaches Jim, and shakes his hand. Al says something in a low voice and leads Jim over to a chair.

I back out of the room and close the door. I lean into the wall outside Al Davis's owner's box and feel my heart thumping. I know I haven't exactly brokered an international peace treaty or put together a multi-billion-dollar trade agreement. All I've done is arrange for two football legends to spend some time together, to have a long overdue conversation, but it feels so much more than that. I've *connected* the two. I feel ridiculously pumped and disproportionately triumphant. I know of only one other person who will understand this feeling. Andrew. I call him.

"I know how you feel, babe," he says. "It's awesome, isn't it? Hey, don't you wanna be in there? Don't you wanna be a fly on the wall?"

"No," I say, and I honestly don't. "I'm just glad I could get them in the same room."

"So, connecting them," Andrew says. "That was the thrill for you?"

"It was huge. That's what I'm saying. Just putting them together. That's the best part. I don't need anything more."

"Yeah, babe! You got the bug," Andrew says. "There's very few of us, JT. Very few."

———

A few weeks later, in fall 2003, I get a call from Andrew on a Saturday evening, not a usual time. With two young kids, Julie and I rarely go out, and Andrew knows this. Andrew and I have become tighter than ever, if that's possible. In addition to our frequent phone calls that can sometimes go for an hour, we manage to see each other every month or so, either crashing in San Antonio, where we always take in a Spurs game or two, or meeting up on the road at big-time sporting events, such as the NBA finals, the Baseball All-Star Game, or the World Series. Andrew's social life has changed, too. Life still seems like a twenty-four-hour tailgate party with nonstop barbecue and burritos, but Andrew has recently found a steady girlfriend, Sandra, a woman I like. She seems into Andrew, shares his love of partying, digs his dogs, and enjoys Andrew's tight rat pack of friends, his so-called wrecking crew, among them but not limited to Jeff Rowe, Michael Drescher, and Bruce Allen. Andrew and I never hesitate to call each other, no matter when. Still, I'm surprised when I pick up the phone and hear his voice Saturday, right before dinner.

"Hey," he says. "Got a minute?"

"Always."

"Couple things."

"Shoot."

"Kinda big."

"Okay."

"So, number one, me and Sandra, looks like we're moving ahead pretty fast. Like she's moving in."

"Wow. Beautiful. Excellent, man. That's really great. You two seem good together."

"Thanks, yeah, I think so, too. She grounds me, keeps me sane."

"I gotta plan a trip there so we can celebrate. I'll bring Julie. What weekend works for you?"

"That's thing number two. You don't have to come here. I'm coming there."

I hear something in his voice that I can't identify. A hesitation. An unusual intake of breath.

"Okay, great, when?"

"Next week." And then Andrew pauses. "I'm moving there."

"Here? To L.A.?"

"I got a new job. My title, technically, is vice president and general manager of Fox Sports Radio."

A chasm opens between us.

A silence.

And then the silence seals up, replaced by the thunderous beating of my heart. I feel literally flooded with joy.

"Holy fucking *shit*. You're gonna be my *boss*."

"Well, yeah, I will."

"This is unbelievable. Phenomenal. Tremendous news. You'll be running the network."

"Yeah, we gotta do some things, get the costs down, revamp the weekend lineup, bunch of stuff."

"Hey, man, I couldn't be happier for you. And for me."

He roars. "I know, right? It's *awesome*."

After we hang up, I stand by the phone digesting the news. Julie appears in the doorway.

I turn to her. "Andrew's moving to L.A. He's gonna be running the network."

"So I gathered," Julie says. "That's great."

"Oh, it's perfect." I pause. "Big surprise, huh? I had no idea this was coming. Weird. He never told me." I pause again. I look down and see that I've knotted the telephone cord. "Why do you think he didn't tell me?"

"Because as of now, he's your boss."

"Right. That'll be great. Don't you think?"

She lifts her shoulders in the tiniest shrug. "It'll be different." She absently fluffs her mane of blonde hair, a move that tells me she's trying to select the right words to say. "You have to be prepared."

I don't hear her.

"Different? Nah, it won't be different. We're tight. Andrew and me, we're unbelievably close." I untangle the phone cord, straighten it out, and say, "I just wonder why he didn't tell me."

11.

The Best Man

Los Angeles
2004–2007

ANDREW AND SANDRA find a rental home not far from us, a small one-level bungalow at the end of a cul-de-sac, backed up beneath a freeway, the house obscured in the shadows of a larger house in front of it. When I come over for the first time, I'm surprised by how nondescript the house is and how difficult it is to find. It feels temporary, as if Andrew hasn't quite committed yet to Los Angeles, or as if he's hiding out. It certainly doesn't seem like the residence of the vice president and general manager of Fox Sports Radio, the guy whose former home in the San Antonio suburbs was known as the major party palace and who once described his taste in decorating to me as "grand."

I figure that Andrew is biding his time, settling in, getting used to the L.A. landscape before he and Sandra move on to some place more permanent and lavish. They bring in just enough furniture to make do, the centerpiece an overstuffed armchair that he plops in front of a wide-screen TV so he can watch his beloved Green Bay Packers on cable.

At first they spend most weekends at our house. Sandra and Julie blend pitchers of margaritas in the kitchen while Andrew and I barbecue outside, keeping an eye on Johnny, who's into playing NASCAR on his tricycle, while Jason totters around, imitating his big brother as best he can. Andrew, the perfect uncle, is riveted by the kids, ready to pounce and pick up Jason should he fall and play pit crew every time Johnny wipes out in the middle of a hairpin turn.

"These kids, babe, the best," Andrew says one fall day, sitting in the backyard, watching me right Johnny's NASCAR tricycle and put him back on the seat.

"Nothing like it," I say.

"You're a great dad," Andrew says.

"Thanks. That means a lot. And you're Uncle Buck."

He laughs and we clink beer bottles.

———

Andrew throws himself into his work, blowing into the office each day like a hurricane. He sweeps his employees up in his energy, his warmth, his stories, his creativity, his larger-than-life presence. Andrew also connects to his staff by e-mail. He e-mails freely and often, beginning each day with a quote, a wise or inspirational saying from a poet, philosopher, politician, writer, or businessperson.

The atmosphere at Fox changes. Everyone in the building—everyone who comes in contact with Andrew—finds his positive attitude infectious and buys into his "anything is possible" and "dare to be great" approach to work and to life. They've signed up with him, committed to taking what seems to be an exciting, upbeat ride. As a producer friend tells me, "It's amazing. Andrew has completely changed things around here. It's not like a business anymore. It's like a big family."

Within a short time, Andrew accumulates a new group of close friends, whom I see more as followers, hangers-on, and wannabes than real friends. I'm not sure he sees them the same way. *It goes with the territory*, I tell myself. I suppose this is what's called the downside of being charismatic.

Then the powers that be move my time slot from a four o'clock start to seven, finishing at midnight. By the time I come in to do my show, Andrew has left for the day. And because Andrew spends almost every second locked away at work, overseeing programming, stuck on conference calls, and attending back-to-back meetings, we curtail our phone calls to each other. We see each other even less. I begin to feel a real void. For the first time, I miss Andrew.

—

February 2004.

Houston.

Super Bowl XXXVIII.

The Carolina Panthers take on the New England Patriots in what Peter King of *Sports Illustrated* will call "the greatest Super Bowl of all time," the Patriots winning 32–29 on Adam

Vinatieri's field goal with four seconds left. The game also features the most controversial halftime show ever, in which Justin Timberlake, singing a duet with Janet Jackson, accidentally or purposely rips open her blouse, exposing her breast to 140 million people watching on television worldwide in what will be called famously a "wardrobe malfunction."

Unfortunately, I miss seeing the game and Janet Jackson's breast.

Instead I spend Super Bowl week working two shows and visiting Andrew in a hospital room, at the bedside of a new Fox employee.

In his typically "grand" style, despite continuous corporate budget concerns, Andrew arranges for essentially the entire Fox Sports Radio network to broadcast from Houston for the run-up to the game and then to attend the game itself. We arrive the Sunday before, check into our hotel rooms, and in the evening crowd into Andrew's suite for the launch of what we all foresee as a week of company bonding and intense partying.

"We got a lot of work to do this week," Andrew says, raising his glass. "But this is our first night here. Sunday before the Super Bowl. Let's get after it, everybody."

He downs a shot, pours another, and the party begins. We match shot for shot and drunken toast for toast, bringing the new guy, a former high school football player, into our circle. I stagger back to my room sometime early the next morning, yanking the blackout curtains tight across the window to block out the rising sun. I sleep until noon, shake off my hangover, and spend a leisurely day hanging with friends and affiliates before I broadcast my show from Radio Row. The next morning

Andrew phones me. "I got a call from the new guy. He's sick. He can't get out of bed. He thinks it's indigestion. He sounded like shit."

By the end of the day, the new guy's self-diagnosed indigestion intensifies and Andrew checks him into the hospital.

After I grab breakfast Tuesday morning, I call Andrew to check in. "How's he doing?"

"Terrible." Andrew lowers his voice. "It's not indigestion. Turned out to be heart trauma."

"Holy shit."

"It gets worse. They did some kind of procedure and it didn't go well. I'm worried."

A muffled voice announcing a doctor's name over a PA system echoes through the phone.

"Where are you?" I say.

"In the hallway outside his room."

"You're at the *hospital*?"

"I'm not leaving him. I'm his boss. What if something happens? Uh-uh. Not on my watch. I will leave no man behind."

I check my watch. I still have several hours before I'm due to go on the air. "I'll keep you company," I say.

For the rest of the week, Andrew spends most of his time sitting by the new guy's bedside. Each night I finish work, catch a few hours of sleep, scarf down some breakfast, and pop in to see Andrew at the hospital. By the end of the week the new guy's wife arrives and his condition improves. Andrew and I are both wasted. I decide to bail on the game and watch it from my living room in L.A.

I head down to the lobby to check out of the hotel and grab a cab to the airport. Andrew waits for me at the front desk. "Hey, babe, thanks for checking in with me at the hospital. You're a good man."

He throws his arms around me in a classic Ashwood rib-crunching bear hug.

—

"You gotta get into NASCAR," Andrew tells me. "It's pretty much untapped territory for radio and I want Fox to get into the sport hard. I'm telling you, auto racing is the best. But you gotta see it for yourself."

I don't question Andrew but I remain skeptical. Any sport that doesn't involve a ball or a puck or two guys pounding the crap out of each other feels like, well, not a sport.

The last Sunday in February, Andrew and I head down to Daytona Beach, Florida, for the Daytona 500, called both the Great American Race and the Super Bowl of Stock Car Racing. We park our rental in the media parking lot, flash our credentials at a line of bouncers who look like oversize race-car drivers with attitude, and enter the grounds of the speedway, swept up in throngs of people dressed like race-car drivers themselves, most lugging coolers filled with beer. As we walk and weave in and out of what seems like thousands of people, Andrew drapes an arm across my shoulders. "You will not believe this event," he says.

Inside the racetrack, Andrew steers me to the merchandise area, marked by a battalion of 18-wheelers, each representing an individual driver. "Gotta pick out your driver," Andrew says.

"That's how this works. You have to choose someone and buy all his gear. You gotta *represent*. I got Matt Kenseth. Wisconsin guy."

"Dale Earnhardt Jr.," I say, more because his is one of the few names I know. "He will dominate."

"Oh, obviously," Andrew says, shooting me an eye roll. "He's a lock."

We join our respective driver's mobs, pull out credit cards, wave them over our heads as we're shoved forward. I come out of the pack thirty minutes later with a hundred dollars' worth of swag—T-shirts, caps, toys for my kids, cup holders, and a six-pack of beer.

We move to the infield, an expanse of grass that seems to go as far as I can see, wide and long as three football fields. A full-out party has broken out, reminding me of the kind of crazy scene that occurred on the lawn of the DK house the first day of every spring, beginning at noon, exploding into the next day. Here RVs sit parked side by side, each with a tricked-out barbecue, the smell of grilling hamburgers piercing the air, kids and adults splashing in portable plastic swimming pools, Lynyrd Skynyrd, Kid Rock, and AC/DC rumbling out of each vehicle. I feel as if I've fallen into a portrait of red-blooded Americana, hard-core, unabashed, unashamed, in the midst of a huge, possibly ignored landscape. As some elitist L.A.–to–New York traveler once called the mass of humanity around me, "the people we fly over."

With the infield party blaring at our backs we walk to the racetrack itself and stop at the final curve, where, as Andrew explains, tradition invites us to sign our names on the finish line. We do so with Sharpies. and then, buzzed from the heat, the beer, and the sheer excitement of the *scene*, we ease over to our luxury box—only one of three or four in the entire place separated by glassed-in partitions—surrounded by two hundred thousand equally buzzed people jacked to get the race started.

We stand for the anthem and then remain on our feet as a roar above us shakes the entire structure of the stadium and the seats of the racetrack.

"Air Force One," Andrew says.

He winks, knowing something.

And then in quick succession, as the race cars rev and waggle to their start positions, men wearing sunglasses and suits sweep into the luxury box next to ours. One of them leads in a German shepherd who sniffs each inch of the place until his handler declares the premises clean. President George W. Bush, waving to the crowd, appears at the starting line and calls out, "Gentlemen, start your engines!" The crowd roars, the party swells into a higher gear, and President Bush and his phalanx of Secret Service guys arrive in the luxury box next to ours. He waves and I think mouths, "How you doing?" I'm not sure. I'm too knocked on my ass by the moment and the swirl of activity and the surreal nature of it all to be sure. I know I wave back and I feel Andrew pounding my back gleefully. "Told you NASCAR was great," he says.

Eventually, the President will leave before the race ends.

He won't have the pleasure of witnessing my driver, Dale Earnhardt Jr., win the Daytona 500 for his dad.

Something happens.

I don't know when it happens, or how, or what causes it.

I can't even put my finger on what "it" is.

But something happens between Andrew and me.

Subtly, almost imperceptibly, without any sign or warning or incident, our friendship starts to fray, and then begins to rip apart.

We stop calling each other every day, cut back to every other day or so, and then we limit our formerly long, intense phone conversations to quick check-ins once or twice a week. We stop hanging out on weekends—Andrew often has other plans, usually work related, and except for the Super Bowl in Houston, where he spent most of his time keeping vigil in a hospital room, and the Daytona 500, we don't go on many road trips.

I don't know if Andrew feels our closeness fading the way I do. We certainly don't talk about it. Even if I wanted to say something to him, his schedule seems so booked that I can't see when we would find a free moment.

I have to deal with it, I know that. And so I do.

In fact, I do what I do best.

I throw myself into my work and try not to think about it.

I'm great at selling and cold-calling.

I excel at *avoiding*.

Maybe I act more sullen or short-fused or testy at home, because after a while Julie confronts me head-on. "You haven't been talking to Andrew so much, have you?"

"Yeah, no, I know. It's been tough. He has a brutal schedule."

I pause.

"And you were right. Since he became my boss, it's different.

He's been hiring new people, working with them, mentoring them. Very time-consuming. Plus he's surrounded himself with a bunch of new friends. Yeah, it's different."

"Do you feel left out?"

I do. Completely. I feel like a fifth wheel.

"Me? No. Not at all. I get it. He's running the whole network. Things had to change. It was inevitable. Part of the deal. It's okay. It's fine. I got a lot on my plate, too. Lot on my plate."

Shut up now, I say to myself. *You're rambling like an idiot.*

Julie looks at me for a long time without speaking.

"What?" I finally say.

"Nothing. I'm a little concerned, that's all."

"About my job?"

"No. About you."

———

I don't spend much time dwelling on the shift in my relationship with Andrew, but I can't lie. I miss how we talked every day—twice a day—about everything and everyone. I miss how we put everything on the table. I never held back. I whined, bitched, moaned, gossiped, and goofed on people who drove both of us crazy. I hate that I can't go there with him anymore. It wouldn't be *professional*. And so I don't.

Mostly, I feel loss. I don't say anything. I'm a *guy*. I suck it up, keep my feelings inside. On the few occasions that I actually make it into work during the day and I see him laughing with some new on-air talent whom I know casually, I do feel left out. Worse, I feel replaced.

I dismiss it. I let it go. I chalk it up to work pressure. I believe that at some point this will turn around. Things will settle down—life will resume—and our friendship will return to the way it was.

And then, before I know it, years pass.

———

June 2007.

I'm gonna be fired.

At the ungodly hour of eight thirty in the morning I drive down Ventura Boulevard toward the squat glass building on the corner of Sepulveda Boulevard, the home of Fox Radio, where I broadcast my radio show every night. I'm heading in to meet Andrew. I take a gulp of my large coffee, return it to the cup holder, grip the steering wheel until my knuckles fade to pale, and say aloud, "I can't believe it. One of my closest friends in the world is about to fire me."

Why else would he shoot me this e-mail first thing?

"Stop by the office today or call me when you get up."

Oh, yeah. No doubt. I'm gone. He's gonna can me.

Either that or he's finally gonna apologize for not inviting me to his wedding.

Yes, I'm still pissed about that. No, not pissed. Hurt. At least that's what my mom used to say when I was like five and I did something to upset her.

"John, I cannot believe you said that to your sister."

"Are you mad?"

"No, I'm not mad. I'm *hurt*. I'm very disappointed in you."

Which of course made me feel worse than if she had said she was pissed. Hurt your mom? Or hurt somebody close to you? That absolutely *wrecks* you.

So, yeah, Andrew, I'm not pissed.

I'm hurt.

Actually, I don't even know what I am anymore. Hurt, pissed, or a combination. I know I was blind with pain. When I found out that I didn't get a wedding invite, I went rip-shit ballistic. Especially when I heard who *was* invited to your exclusive, super-secret, apparently spur-of-the-moment wedding in Cabo, only your favorite place on earth. Your blessed event happened so fast you'd think you *had* to get married. Bottom line, you invited your tight wrecking crew of longtime friends, your core group of guys like Jeff and Dresch and Timm, and a select few of your new friends from the network. But you left me out. I didn't make the cut. Here's the strangest part. If you had taken a poll of your friends, I guarantee they would've all pegged *me* to be your best man. You didn't even tell me you were getting married. I found out through the office grapevine, from the in-house chatter, the bagel-table buzz. I happened to pop into work one morning—dropped in to see you, no reason, it had just been forever since we saw each other—and Jen, your secretary, *informed* me that you weren't in, that you had taken the week off. The way she whirled around and starting typing on her computer, I knew that I wasn't getting anything else out of her, no specifics, so I drifted into the bull pen, nosed around, and found out from I forget who—Looney, maybe—that you were getting freaking *married*. I think I felt my legs go slack or I went into momentary shock because the next thing I knew

I was behind the wheel of the SUV, driving down Ventura, heading home in a kind of fog. I blew into the house and told Julie about the wedding and even she—calm, even-keeled, the woman who has never spoken an unkind word about anybody except maybe a serial killer or a politician who got caught banging an intern or texting pictures of his junk—admitted that the non-invite stumped her.

Then she put it all together for me.

"To be honest? You two haven't been close for a while."

That was true.

"You hardly see each other."

True, too.

I picked up the morning's newspapers, pulled out the sports section, and dropped the rest into the recycling bin by the back door. "That's because Andrew gets to his office first thing in the morning when I'm sleeping and leaves before I roll in. I start my shift at seven. I don't have any reason to go into the studio during the day. We don't keep the same hours."

"Ships passing in the night," Julie said.

"We used to see him every weekend," I said. "I can't remember the last time he came over."

"It's been a while."

"You were right. It's been really tough straddling that line between my boss and my friend. The stupid line keeps moving."

Driving to work, I stop at a red light at Woodman, a few blocks from the studio, and I change my mind.

He's not gonna fire me.

No way. It makes no sense. Andrew loves my show. He e-mailed me a few weeks ago to tell me how great I was doing.

He had been listening to me on Military Night, a special feature I put together with his encouragement after the events of September 11. Every Thursday I invite a serviceman or servicewoman stationed in Iraq or Afghanistan to phone in. They go to the head of the line and I put them right on the air. I'm passionate about our troops and celebrate them whenever I can. He loves that, loves my passion in all things. He also mentioned how good I sounded with Tomm Looney, my cohost. Andrew came up with the idea of putting us together. I remember when he broke that news to me. He called me into a meeting that time, too.

"You're very intense, very driven," Andrew said. "And that obviously comes through on the air. I don't want to change that. But I know you off the air and I know you're also a lot of fun. I want that side of you to come out, too."

"Okay," I said, furrowing my forehead intensely, not sure where this was going. "How?"

"I'm putting you together with Tomm Looney. I think the two of you will complement each other. I got a feeling Looney will lighten you up."

Andrew, never one to settle, liked to tinker around. And when he did, he did so with a flourish. He took chances. He reminded me of a wild orchestra director, shoulder-length hair flying, fingers flicking the baton crazily, knifing through the air. A mad genius of radio.

I'll admit when Andrew told me about Looney, I wasn't sure. Looney was currently the announcer for *The Best Damn Sports Show Period*, a hot nightly show on Fox TV, and while he seemed to take sports seriously he also appeared to be a cutup.

I didn't see how we would fit. Plus, I'd been on my own forever. My last partner on the radio was Pete Rose, years ago. I had gotten used to doing my show alone. I liked the freedom, the free-form way I could approach my show without having to think about how I would mesh with another personality. Now I had to worry about finding that vague, elusive quality called chemistry. But I trusted Andrew. I trusted his experience, his vast knowledge, and his instinct, especially when it came to me. If Andrew said, "Jump, I got you," I didn't hesitate. I knew that he would catch me if I fell. So when Andrew told me he was teaming me up with Looney, I hesitated only briefly, and then I went all in.

Looney came into the studio the next day, we shook hands, and even though we both understood that we would still be doing *The JT the Brick Show*, I welcomed him as my cohost. I told him we had to commit 100 percent or else it wouldn't work. He agreed. We laughed because we both felt like Andrew had fixed us up on a blind date.

It worked. Andrew got it right. Looney and I have been partners going on four years.

Maybe he's gonna make some kind of change to my show, I think as I sit behind the wheel of the SUV waiting for the light to change at Woodman. *Maybe he wants to tinker with something else, try a new direction.*

The light goes green. I pull into the left lane, drive a few blocks, and try to empty my mind of all possibilities. No sense theorizing. I'll find out the reason for the meeting soon enough.

I turn into the parking structure, swipe my key card, which raises the metal bar blocking my way into the designated parking area, drive inside the shadowy garage, find a space, park, and head into the building. I enter the bull pen, say hi to a couple of producers I know and an update guy I've worked with, and then, putting my head down like a running back, whip around the corner to Andrew's office.

Through the glass wall, I can see Andrew inside. He sits at his desk in his high, black leather chair, his massive back turned toward the door. He types ferociously on his computer, probably pounding out an e-mail. I tap on his open door and move into his office. Without waiting for him to spin around or acknowledge me, I slide into the chair facing his desk. The chair squeaks as I sit down. He doesn't say a word, doesn't acknowledge me, doesn't offer a hi, a sigh, or a grunt.

As he types, I take in the furnishings in the office—the leather love seat in the corner, the skinny twin chrome floor lamps, the flat-screen TV mounted on the wall, and his personal wall of fame, selected photographs of his life, many featuring his beloved Green Bay Packers, including a framed collage of photos from Super Bowls. Then I follow along the wall of photos as if I'm at a photography exhibit. I take in a picture of Andrew and former Washington Redskins Hall of Fame coach George Allen—Bruce's dad—and a group of photos of Andrew and his closest friends, Andrew with other sports celebrities, and then several photographs of the two of us, including one with our arms around each other at the Final Four and another near the track at the Daytona 500.

I study this gallery of photographs and I say nothing.

I wait.

Andrew keeps typing.

Finally, after what feels like five minutes of electric silence, he swivels around in his chair and faces me. He looks pale. He frowns and his cheeks seem to fold in. Still he says nothing. He simply stares. And then he scoots to the edge of his chair, hoists his massive 300-pound frame, rises to his feet, and, moving faster than you would think a man of his bulk could move, goes to the door and closes it. He rumbles back to his desk, looks at me again briefly, and lowers himself back into his chair. The chair groans. Andrew leans forward.

"I have some news," he says.

He pauses, then appears to gather himself. He looks off, perhaps searching for the strength to continue or the right words to say.

"Okay," I say. "What's going on?"

He licks his lips and looks slightly past me as he speaks, his hands waving, animated. "I haven't been feeling well for a while, probably since my last trip to San Antonio. I get this burning sensation every time I eat. It's been…alarming. I got concerned."

I nod.

He swallows, frowns. "I checked myself into the hospital for some tests."

He locks his eyes on me.

"Looks like I have cancer."

He speaks these words without emotion, almost in a kind of measured monotone, the way a news anchor delivers the lead story.

"I'm gonna get a second opinion, maybe a *third* opinion. I'm gonna talk to the Mays family in San Antonio, then head down

215

to MD Anderson in Houston to talk to some folks there. The people at Fox have been wonderful, very supportive. But—" He sniffs, lowers his gaze to the blotter on his desk, then raises his head and locks his eyes into mine again. "The tests came back pretty clear. It's cancer. Pancreatic."

I blink and my breath comes rapidly. I feel as if I'm panting.

And then I'm gone, floating out of my body, away from myself, away from *here*, as if I'm sitting in a movie theater watching the two of us on the screen sitting in this office, talking across the desk. Everything in this room feels unreal. The furniture looks oversize and distorted. The photos on the wall flip upside down and start to shimmer.

I want to walk back into the office again. I want to redo this moment. I want Andrew to turn to me and tell me he's moving my time slot or cutting my hours or adding a third cohost. I want Andrew to tell me I'm *fired*. I just don't want to hear this. I can't be hearing this.

Andrew licks his lips again and keeps his stare fastened on me.

"I need your help," he says softly.

I click back to reality, my body quivering, poised to lunge at this unknown something, to strike it down, to protect Andrew. Everything I felt on the drive over, the anger and hurt and confusion about the wedding, the concern about our friendship changing, eroding—all of it—falls away. I want to tell Andrew that I forgive everything, but that feels selfish and one-sided. But I do forgive him. I know that he forgives me, too. And I know that we have just rushed past the place where our relationship got stuck. We have transcended that and arrived somewhere new.

"Anything," I say. "You got it. Whatever you need."

"Thank you. That's why I called you in. I know I can trust you. I know I can count on you."

"Totally. A hundred percent."

He sighs, folds his hands on his desk, and stares at them as if looking for clarity in the curves of his knuckles. "This is all new. We're just figuring it out. Sandra will be running point, of course, but I'm gonna ask you to be the main go-to guy whenever I need you to help me out. Doctor's appointments, whatever...you know."

His voice trails off into his desk.

"Lot of decisions," he says, undoing his clasped hands and pressing his palms into his blotter. He blinks. "This is the biggest fight of my life. Winning is my only option."

I nod again, a player receiving his coach's impassioned half-time pep talk. I bring my hands to my mouth. My fingertips have gone ice-cold.

"Don't say anything about this, except to Julie. I want to keep this a private matter for now."

"Absolutely."

"Good. So. Okay. Once I have more information, I'll let you know the next step."

He slaps his desk and springs to his feet. I stand at the same time, as if shot out of my seat. Andrew circles around his desk and spreads his arms. It looks as if his hands could reach all the way to each wall. He throws his arms around me, hugging me only the way he can, with all his might, completely enclosing me. I hug him back. We hold on to each other, clinging to each other, knowing that in the matter of ten minutes, without saying a word, we have dropped every ounce of bullshit that has ever existed between us.

"I love you," he says.

"I love you, too."

I feel his hand gently patting my back.

"It's gonna be okay," he says.

"It will. I know it will."

"Thanks for being there," Andrew says.

We pull away.

Andrew heads back around to his desk and cozies up to his computer. I assume my running back position—head down, shoulder lowered—and barrel into the door. I rush through the bull pen, out of the building, into the parking structure, and climb into the SUV. I turn on the ignition and allow myself a moment to catch my breath. I look at my hand, then turn it over. I see no sign of trembling. That's what Andrew needs. A steady hand. He needs me to be a rock. I will try to be. No. I will be.

I don't allow myself to imagine what lies ahead for him. I can't go there. I need to digest this new reality and take it one step at a time. I laugh for half a second. *One step at a time.* What a cliché. I guess that's how clichés are born, from the truth.

I pull out of the parking structure and ease back onto Ventura Boulevard heading the opposite way now, home to Julie, to break the news to her that Andrew has cancer and that he has designated me to be there with him, by his side, his go-to guy, as he fights for his life.

It occurs to me then that he may not have invited me to his wedding, but he has just asked me to be his best man.

12.

Thirteen Months

Los Angeles
November 2007–November 2008

AND SO IT BEGAN.

   My tutorial with Andrew.

   The crash course about life—about how to live—that we managed to cram in over the next thirteen months.

   As I said, I didn't keep a journal or jot down notes or speak into a tape recorder. If I had been more conscious then that Andrew was taking this time to try to teach me some things, I would have at least kept a legal pad with me and scribbled down what he said. But after that day in his office, I felt that he had merely assigned me a special role in his fight for his life and that was all.

   At first, strangely, I saw this as a kind of two-sided opportunity: the chance for him, with me at his side, to win the fight for his life, and the chance for us to renew our friendship. I saw us getting closer through cancer. I was honored that he chose me, that he trusted me, that he needed me. I didn't know that he also wanted to teach me. Maybe he didn't know it, either.

As I look back, I realize that while Andrew truly felt that he would win, that he would survive, he also felt a sense of urgency. I did, too. I kept my career going, riding my night show hard, cranked up to its usual fever pitch, but somehow I managed to blast through my show those months on some kind of autopilot. In some sense I always erase each show I do, on purpose, starting fresh with the next one. But I have less recall than usual of the shows I did over those thirteen months. It's as if another part of me, or an avatar, a second JT the Brick, pulled it together to do a nightly sports talk radio show. I was of course preoccupied, distracted in a way I had never been before, and that I can't imagine ever being again.

While I exploded through my night show in a kind of high-pitched fury, I did my best to maintain an even keel when I was with Andrew during the day. I tried to be as attentive to him as possible, attempted to absorb his progress, his process, and eventually— later—the lessons he taught me.

As I look back at those thirteen months, what I feel now is a kind of frenzy. Everything felt contracted, moving at a much faster pace. And every moment seemed critical. Life seemed loaded. At a certain point, perhaps sooner rather than later, I think Andrew and I both knew that he was running out of time.

Now it all feels like a blur.

13.

Driving Andrew

"It's Not About You"

ANDREW'S DIAGNOSIS HAS changed. During his four sessions of chemotherapy in Houston, after a series of scans and examinations, the doctors at MD Anderson conclude that instead of pancreatic cancer—the treatment of which offers, best case, the hope only of extending his life rather than the possibility of saving his life—Andrew has esophageal cancer. Andrew considers this unexpected turn good news. Committed to continuing his role as the head of Fox Sports Radio as efficiently as possible, Andrew decides to turn his cancer fight into a home game and schedules his next round of chemotherapy in Los Angeles at City of Hope. He puts me on alert and tells me to block off the entire day one upcoming Monday. Using a sports reference the way we always do, Andrew asks me to go into the bull pen and warm up. I will soon be entering the game.

With the discovery of this cancer comes a different treatment philosophy, which Andrew calls *shrinkage*. Simply put, Andrew will undergo a brutal, aggressive regimen of chemotherapy and radiation with the goal of reducing the cancerous tumors to a size small enough for the doctors to remove them surgically. Andrew attacks every day with that purpose—shrinkage.

"So, in this one case, shrinkage is good," Andrew says to Julie and me at our house Sunday, the day before I drive him for his first chemotherapy session at City of Hope.

We have gone back to having Andrew and Sandra over frequently, barbecuing and hanging out many weekend afternoons. Today, in early November, with the omnipresent low hazy cloud layer turning the San Fernando Valley unseasonably cool, he trudges slowly into the house, as if conserving his energy, bundled up in a bulky sweater, heavy coat, and fur-lined Uggs boots. His hair, rock-star long a few months ago, dusting his shoulders, now sits close cropped, military short. He hugs Julie, hugs me, takes the bottle of water I hand to him, and swivels his head toward Johnny and Jason's bedroom. "Where are they?"

"Out back," Julie says. "They're into football today."

"And their favorite team?" Andrew says, raising his eyebrows in expectation.

"The team Daddy works for," I say. "Raiders."

Andrew howls, wounded. "What? Are you insane? PACKERS! You have to raise these kids right, otherwise you don't know what could happen. They could become social deviants or hard-core criminals or worse. They could go into radio. I gotta talk to them."

Andrew takes a careful swig of his water and frowns. I drop my head. It hurts to see how hard it is for him to swallow.

"Boys," he calls weakly as he heads outside. I follow, clutching a beer.

We find Johnny, seven, and Jason, five, in the backyard running pass patterns, taking turns as quarterback and receiver. Andrew steps onto the lawn and spreads his arms. My sons howl and charge him and Andrew engulfs them both in a bear hug. After a few seconds, Andrew's body sags, and my sons unclench from his grasp. Andrew wheezes a little, composes himself, and then snatches the ball from Jason, waves at Johnny to go deep, and heaves a pass that wobbles in his approximate direction, falling short. Johnny dives for it futilely and slaps the ground. "I should've had it," he says, which breaks Andrew up.

Andrew and I find two chairs in the shade and for the next ten minutes sit silently watching my kids throw passes or hand the ball off to each other and then dodge, weave around, and stiff-arm imaginary opponents and each other. Andrew loses himself in their play, cheering them on, clapping, throwing his arms up in the touchdown signal.

"Awright!" I shout. I put my beer down, shoot out of my chair, and dive into the action. I grab Jason, flip him upside down, and dance out for a pass. Johnny tosses the ball to me. I gather it in one-handed, free Jason, and run at both kids in slow motion. They grab me, swarm me, tackle me, and then, falling to my knees, I allow them to drag me to the ground and climb all over me.

"Personal foul." I huff from my prone position on the grass. "Piling on, too many kids on a father, fifteen *yards*."

"Bad call," Johnny calls, straddling me. He and Jason step over me. I reach toward them, asking them to haul me up. I grab their hands and pull them down. The kids scream and Andrew roars. Then shouting, "I give!" I make my way back to my chair next to Andrew.

"I love watching you with them," he says. "You're a great dad."

I go quiet, remembering that he said this to me one other time, years ago, when he first moved to Los Angeles.

"I learned from the best," I say after a while, and then I add, "I had a good childhood."

"Me, too." Andrew looks at Johnny and Jason, who giggle, toss the football, and tackle each other.

"They will remember this," he says, and then turns to me with surprising urgency. "Never forget your childhood. Even the bad stuff. It's who you are."

———

The next day I pull the SUV into Andrew's driveway and climb out to escort him to the car. The second I step foot on the pavement his dogs go nuts inside, the two of them barking and growling like I'm an intruder or the UPS guy. Andrew's voice, dancing through an open window, as smooth and mellow as it was when he did morning drive in Milwaukee years ago calling himself BJ Hunter, soothes them, crooning, "It's okay, stop it, it's only JT," and then the front door whips open and Andrew, wearing his heavy coat and his Uggs, a leather pouch slung over his shoulder, moves toward me. He walks slowly and smiles when he sees me, his eyes sparkling. "Yeah, babe," he says. "Let's do this."

I run around to the passenger side, open the door, and reach for his shoulder bag.

"I got it," he says.

"You sure? Because it looks kind of heavy—"

"It's only my laptop. I can handle it."

He climbs into the SUV, lands on the seat with a loud *whap*, clears his throat, puffs out two ragged breaths, and then sighs to settle himself. I hurry around to the driver's side, strap in, and back out of the driveway.

"You know how to go?" Andrew says, slipping on sunglasses even though the morning cloud cover hovers low like a lumpy gray blanket.

I tap the sun visor above the steering wheel. "Printed out directions. We're all set."

"Beautiful."

Andrew stabs a stubby finger at the radio, which I have tuned to our station on Fox. The morning guys come on, the lead-ins to Jim Rome. They're talking about what fun they had over the weekend. They howl, break each other up. One laughs all the way through a not remotely funny story about a starlet he tried to pick up at a party he crashed at some celebrity's Malibu hideaway.

I grunt. "I thought you tuned to Fox *Sports* Radio. Be nice to hear some fucking sports." I talk louder, directly into the car radio. "Tell me about yesterday's NFL games. There were only about a million pivotal games. Talk to me about *sports*."

Andrew laughs, then his laugh dissolves into a cough. He

grimaces and gently rubs his throat. Finally, his voice slightly raspy, he says, "I actually told them to get more personal. You gotta compete with all the other crazies on morning drive. I got the good hard-core sports at night."

He reaches over and bops me on the shoulder. I look at him. He grins. I shrug. "You're the boss."

"Gotta deal with all types of personalities," he says. "It's like herding cats."

I nod, and settle into the right lane of the four-lane freeway, keeping the ride steady, driving five miles under the speed limit. I poke a finger into the sun visor, feel around for the directions to City of Hope, pull them down, and glance at them. "Okay, yeah. We're good."

"It's pretty much a straight shot," Andrew says.

"Just want to make sure." I tap the steering wheel and feel Andrew's eyes on me. I squint through the windshield, grip the wheel tighter, and slow down.

"You all right?" Andrew says.

"What? Yeah. I'm fine."

Well, in fact, I'm not.

But I don't dare tell him the truth, which is...

I'm nervous.

This is so new, all of it—my role, my responsibility, how I fit into Andrew's cancer, my "job description." He has chosen me because he trusts me and he believes I can handle being his chemotherapy partner.

I want to be that friend. I am honored to be that friend.

I'm just not sure I'm up to it.

And so...I'm nervous.

I'm afraid to . . . I don't know. Fail?

I exhale.

I feel Andrew staring at me. "You sure you're all right?"

"Totally. Why?"

"You're driving like my grandmother."

"I don't want to miss the exit," I say.

"No, you don't want to do that," Andrew says. "You only got about twenty miles. So be alert."

That gets me. I laugh. I pick up speed and move over one lane.

Andrew relaxes. He turns down the radio. After a moment, he says, "Remember when we went to the Rose Bowl a couple years ago?"

I ease my grip on the steering wheel. "Texas, USC," I say. "We ducked out of there with five minutes left and SC ahead by twelve—"

"And of course Vince Young goes nuts and leads Texas back in an *epic* comeback—"

"We missed the greatest Rose Bowl game in history so we could beat the traffic."

And now we're both laughing. I signal, look for an opening, and zip into the fast lane.

"That's all this is, JT," Andrew says, his voice a shade above a whisper. "Me and you. Hanging out. But instead of going to a game or tailgating or hitting a bar the way we used to, we're gonna sit in a room together for a few hours and work, or shoot the shit while I get shot up with some really cool, powerful drugs."

"You make it sound like a party."

"It will be. Exactly. Minus the liquor, loud music, and loose women."

I laugh again, feeling a release.

"Gonna beat this thing," I say suddenly.

"Fucking A. All the way. It's about winning."

We don't say much the rest of the way.

And maybe my adrenaline has kicked in, but the nervousness and fear evaporate and calm descends. I feel focused and controlled. I'm the driver. The quarterback.

I got this now, I think. *I'm more than up for it.*

I realize then that Andrew has taught me an important lesson just by putting me at ease.

It's not about you, I say to myself.

What a concept for a guy who makes his living talking to himself.

I look over at Andrew and catch his eye.

"Gonna win," I say.

He nods, reaches over, and rubs my shoulder.

We exit the freeway.

14.

The First Session

"Make Someone's Day"

Los Angeles
November 2007

WE SIT IN the waiting room, the two of us, on alert for the receptionist to call Andrew into the infusion center to receive his first chemotherapy at City of Hope. Head down, he flips absently through an ancient issue of *Sports Illustrated*. If he's nervous, he doesn't show it, except for a single moment when he whistles out a startlingly loud sigh while snapping the pages of the magazine. I'm jittery, my legs pumping out of control. I place my hands on my knees, push them down to keep them still.

Except for some muffled Muzak blowing down from speakers hidden in the ceiling, silence fills the room. Typical of most waiting rooms, I know, but this silence feels weightier, darker. At least that's how I feel. For confirmation, I scan the other people in the room and take in a collection of solemn pale faces and many heads covered with knit hats. Andrew tosses the magazine onto the chair next to him and trains his eyes on the other side of the room, where I've fastened my focus onto a mom and her young son, a boy around ten years old. I'm guessing at his age because he is completely bald and looks older and sadly alien. The mom and her son look straight ahead, both with eyes pale and lifeless.

Andrew sees me looking at the mom and her son, leans over, and whispers, "How old you think he is? Nine, ten?"

"Right around there, yeah."

Suddenly, Andrew rises to his feet, lumbers across the room, and parks himself in front of the mom and her son. "Looks like we're both in for some fun today, huh?" he says to the boy. "Oh, *yeah.*"

The kid looks away shyly, and then after a second or two turns back and takes in this giant who's kneeling before him. Andrew offers the kid his fist. The kid looks at it uncertainly and then bumps it lightly with his small, loose fist, fingers only halfway tucked.

"Yeah, babe," Andrew says. "I'm Andrew, but you can call me what my friends call me."

He holds, waits for the boy to respond.

"What's that?" the kid says in a tiny voice that comes out just above a squeak.

"Gorilla."

The kid's eyes widen and he repeats, "Gorilla."

"Ever hear of the Green Bay Packers?" Andrew says.

The kid shrugs.

"Yeah, come on, you have."

The kid smiles.

"Anyway, I grew up in a small town in Wisconsin. I loved to play football. Lived for it. When I was your age, all I wanted to do was play for the Packers. My dream, you know? I never made it, but that's okay. I'll always be a Green Bay Packer in my heart. Hey, man, you want some gorilla power?"

The kid hesitates and then he nods. Andrew takes the boy's hand and presses it between both of his. He holds it there for a count of five.

"There you go. That should do it. You feel it? Gorilla power will make you very strong and very tough, even stronger and tougher than you already are. Get you through the bad stuff. It's very fast acting. You feel it yet?"

The kid nods.

"I hope I didn't give you too much. You'll know in a few days if you can't stop eating bananas."

The receptionist calls a name.

"That's us," the kid's mom says. She stands up and puts her arm around her son. "Come on, honey. It's time."

"Don't forget," Andrew says. "You got gorilla power in you. That'll make you strong."

He holds out his fist again. This time the kid slams Andrew's fist harder.

"Ow! See? Now, that's what I'm talking about!"

The kid grins. Standing over him, his mom mouths, "Thank you." Even halfway across the room, where I sit, I can see her quickly wipe away a tear.

The mom and her son disappear into the infusion center. Breathless, Andrew walks slowly back toward me. He sits down heavily on his chair and absently picks up the *Sports Illustrated* he discarded before.

"That was incredible," I say.

Andrew flips through the magazine, pretends he's reading. "You know the expression 'Have a nice day'?"

"Yeah. Of course."

"How do you do that?"

"I'm not sure I—"

Andrew flips the magazine aside again. "You can't control if you're gonna have a nice day. You might be having a shitty day, all day, through no fault of your own. Just the way the day is going."

"Yeah, like, for example, you might be having a whole day of chemotherapy," I say, quietly.

"Yeah. So try to *give* someone a good day. Or at least give someone a good couple of minutes. You can control that."

"Give a good day," I repeat.

The receptionist, a heavy woman in her fifties wearing unflattering Coke-bottle glasses, calls his name.

Andrew slowly gets to his feet. I start to help him off with his coat, but he shivers and tightens the coat around him.

"Cold in here, Heather," he says to the receptionist, reading her name on a plaque in front of her. "You wouldn't have a bottle of tequila stashed in a file drawer back there to warm me up, would you?"

Heather blushes and tries to fight off a smile. "Maybe I can adjust the heat," she says.

"Or you could adjust the heat. Thanks, Heather. You get bored out here, come on back. The party's in my room."

Heather, her face deep red now, laughs. She can't help it. "I'm sure it is."

I push through the double doors and hold them open as Andrew, walking slower than I've ever seen him, starts to plow past me.

"Mr. Ashwood," Heather calls.

He stops and turns back.

"You made my day."

15.

The Second Session

"You're Only as Good as Who You're With"

Green Bay, Wisconsin
December 9, 2007

IN THE FADING late afternoon light, we pull out of the lush grounds of City of Hope, heading back to the freeway. We drive in silence, the only sound Andrew's labored breathing echoing through the car. Finally, he speaks softly. "Can I ask you a favor?"

"Sure. Anything."

"Will you be my information guy? Sandra's covering my family in Wisconsin, but I need you to keep my friends, the wrecking crew, in the loop." Andrew's voice sounds thin and flat, as if the mere act of speaking has knocked the wind out of him.

"Absolutely," I say.

"I'll get you all the contact info. I don't want to say too much, no gory details, just...you know...keep them informed..."

His voice fades. He closes his eyes and leans his head against the passenger window.

Today Andrew has completed his second chemotherapy session. The news of late has been promising. His most recent scan shows evidence of some shrinkage. He has taken the first step toward allowing the doctors an opportunity to remove the tumors. To me Andrew appears at once elated and exhausted, and although he will never admit it and will always try to hide it, his spirits seem for the first time to wilt.

I check the clock on the dashboard. I will have just enough time to drop Andrew off, get home, grab some food, and make it to the studio to start my show at seven. I will have no time to decompress; I'll barely find a moment to catch my breath. I take a few minutes and focus on my show. I consider a couple of topics and then I shift gears and think about what I have going on during the upcoming week. I remember that I'm flying to Oakland Sunday for the Raiders game.

An idea jumps into my head.

I go over my schedule, game by game, making sure I have it right.

Andrew's head jerks forward. "Sorry. I nodded off."

"It's been a long day."

"This bastard is tough," he says. "But I'm tougher."

"You got that right," I say. "It's all about winning."

"Winning."

I pause, and then I blurt, "How do you feel about a road trip?"

"Now? I don't know. Where?"

"Lambeau Field. Packers, Raiders. The Sunday before your next chemo. We'll spend the weekend. Get after it. Party, tailgate, and take in the game. Get everybody up there together. Have a Wisconsin reunion."

It may be the late afternoon light trickling in, but a spattering of color seems to flush through Andrew's face.

"My homecoming," he says.

"You got it."

Andrew rubs his hands together while a wide grin spreads across his face. "I am so *in*."

—◆—

We gather in Green Bay on a frigid Saturday, fifteen of us, a few flying up from L.A., but mostly Andrew's friends and family from Wisconsin—his nephews, Chris and Spencer Stiles; several of his closest pals, Timm Amundson and Matt Miller among them; his college roommate Kipper McGee; and his former boss Jeff McCarthy, who once, long ago, fired him but has remained a good friend, a testament to Andrew as a person. You may end up firing him from your company, but you will still keep him in your life.

The night before the game—thanks to Andrew's nephew Chris—we take over a private room in a restaurant. After dinner we toast Andrew, each of us offering him our support and our prayers. The Raiders arrange for a cameraman and sound guy to travel with us and film the whole weekend, including interviews with each participant. I oversee the editing of hours of footage into a forty-minute souvenir DVD I send to every guy who attends.

At one point during cocktails a large man in a leather jacket strolls into the party. He hesitates and looks around for a familiar face. I catch his eye and excuse myself from the group

I'm with and greet the man at the door. "Thanks for coming, Coach," I say, pumping his hand. "I'm really glad Jay Glazer was able to set this up."

"My pleasure."

"Oh, my God," Andrew says, seeing me at the door with the guy who's just come in. Andrew stands unsteadily, his mouth flapped open like a trapdoor. "I don't believe it. Mike McCarthy."

"Yeah, babe," the coach of the Green Bay Packers says. The room explodes with laughter, and then we all applaud.

"How you doing, Andrew?" the coach says.

"Hanging in," Andrew says.

"We're pulling for you, the whole team. We all send you our thoughts and prayers. This guy"—McCarthy says to the room, pointing at Andrew, who makes his way toward him—"is *the* number one Packers fan. Without a doubt."

Andrew throws his arms around the Packers coach and the two big men hug each other.

"Thank you, Coach," Andrew says, his words muffled in McCarthy's shoulder.

"You got it, big guy."

They pull away, gripping each other's forearms.

"You keep fighting," Mike McCarthy says.

"Winning is the only option," Andrew says. He lasers a fierce look of determination into Mike McCarthy's eyes.

"I know we got a few Raiders fans here," the coach says, eyeing me, "but we're gonna win one tomorrow for Andrew."

More applause, handshakes, and another quick bear hug from Andrew, and then Mike McCarthy waves and heads outside. I catch up to him. "That meant the world to him, Coach. You have no idea."

"Glad to do it. He's a special guy."

A few minutes later, we begin a fresh round of toasts and testimonials. I speak briefly, thanking Andrew's friends and family from Wisconsin and the Midwest who have come here to share this evening. Andrew, looking more robust than I have seen him in months, stands in front of all of us. He thanks me and Chris and Spencer for putting this weekend together, saying, "I can't thank you enough, all of you, each one of you in this room...I love you all." He takes a beat and adds, "It's real simple. You're only as good as who you're with."

We cheer and then scatter into small groups and party late into the night. Many guys repeat the same sentiment to me: "Andrew? We're gonna have many, many more years together. The last guy I'm worried about is Andrew Ashwood. He's gonna beat this. I have no doubt."

The next day, adding an exclamation point, the Packers rip the Raiders 38–7 on the frozen tundra of Lambeau Field, to run their season's record to a gaudy 11–2.

The weekend lights Andrew up. The high spirits, camaraderie, and sheer love he felt from all of us carry him as if on a cloud into the next chemotherapy session. As we climb into the SUV for the drive to City of Hope, we break down the weekend.

"Your nephews are tremendous," I say. "And you have awesome friends."

"JT, life is all about your friends and family. Connecting to them and staying connected. They will lift you up. I can't say this enough. You're only as good as who you're with."

16.

The Third Session

"It's Okay to Be Wrong"

Los Angeles
December 2007

HOUR THREE OF chemo, session four.

Antsy today, I have taken two breaks, sipped two cups of black coffee, wandered the grounds, and called Julie, my dad, my agents, Mike Pearson, Looney, Jimmy Baxter, Bobby G., Dresch, and Jeff. And that was just during my *first* break.

I'm not bored or anxious. I'm antsy because I feel helpless.

Andrew, on the other hand, seems content today, propped up in his hospital bed, an IV snagged in his forearm dripping nutrients neck and neck with the stuff designed for shrinkage. He pays no attention to anything but his laptop. He bangs out e-mails, staying connected, scribbling suggestions for his on-air talent, and commenting effusively to the suits—those in power—because lately the numbers look good. Ratings and revenues are on the rise. He's being hailed as a hero and, as always, a force of nature.

Andrew's work ethic inspires me. During break two, I decide that Andrew's hard work is his fuel. It's what is helping him survive. I believe that he is literally working for his life.

As I watch him send off another e-mail, I ask myself, *Would I be able to find that same strength and purpose if the roles were reversed, if I were the one with cancer?*

I think I'd be a basket case. I couldn't handle it. I'd throw in the towel. I don't think I would have Andrew's fight.

But I wonder.

So I ask him.

"If I got sick, do you think I could do it?"

Andrew keeps typing, never takes his eyes off his screen or his keyboard. "Do what?"

"Work the way you do. Stay connected. Keep going. You're fucking amazing."

Andrew stops, peeks at me over the top of his laptop. "What are you saying?"

I scratch my cheek. "I don't know."

"Are you saying that you would give up?"

"I'm not saying that, no, I'm just—"

I swallow the rest because I can't speak the truth that's boring into me.

Yes, I might give up.

Andrew lowers his laptop, revealing a narrow smile that creases his face. "Why do you think you're here?"

Before I can formulate an answer, Andrew raises his voice and practically shouts, "Because you're a fighter, JT," and for emphasis he repeats, "You're a *fighter*. The two of us, babe, we're tag-teaming this bastard."

"Unbelievable. You're giving *me* a pep talk. There's something wrong here."

He roars. "There's nothing wrong. Everything that goes down in this room is exactly the way it should be. Even if it looks upside down or sideways or backwards."

Even if I feel the chemotherapy weighing on me, wearing me down?

I don't say that. The thought shoots through my mind, but I knock it back, keep it from flying out of my mouth. Instead I say, "Sam said something great in Green Bay."

Sam is Sam Betesh, my former producer. Andrew saw great potential in Sam and moved him from my show at night to work days. At the time, I wasn't sure of Andrew's wisdom in this, but the move has worked for everyone, in particular Sam, challenging him and giving his career a boost. Andrew was right. And I admit, I may have been a tad selfish wanting to keep Sam with me at night.

"What did Sam say?" Andrew asks.

"He said that you're the best boss he's ever had."

Andrew shrugs, but I can tell he's pleased.

"The truth is, you know so much. Sam says you seem to know what to do in every situation."

I don't expect Andrew's reaction.

"Well, I don't always know what to do. I do usually have an *opinion*. And I have seen everything…because I've been fired so much. I know exactly what *not* to do. There was a time I got fired from every job I ever had. I was on quite a roll."

And then Andrew's expression changes and he looks at me with a grave seriousness. "You don't always have to be right, JT."

He lets the words sink in.

"In fact, being right can be a curse. You learn way more from your failures than from your successes."

I settle into the chair next to his bed. I suddenly feel less antsy. I sit at the edge of Andrew's hospital bed and take in these words that suddenly seem so crucial for me to hear.

"Of course, you have to try. You have to try to do the right thing. Shoot for the stars, go for broke. I always say, 'Dare to be great.' But if you miss the mark, or you make a mistake, or you're just wrong, it's fine. You'll learn from the experience. I'm living proof."

He pauses one more time.

"It's okay to fuck up. It's okay to be wrong."

17.

The Fourth Session

"There's Always a Way Out"

Los Angeles
December 2007

KNEES BENT, SHOULDERS low, the matronly fifty-something nurse we call Our Lady of the Perpetual Scowl and I prepare to hoist Andrew onto his hospital bed. Andrew has had a rough few days. The skin on his face appears loose and sallow and his breathing comes rapidly in soft, labored gasps. A few moments ago, pushing through the double doors of the infusion center, he wobbled and started to teeter. I reached out, grabbed his arm, and steadied him. He winced, looked at me in momentary confusion, and then grunted and allowed me to guide him past the nurses' station and into his room.

Although he's weak, he's still heavy, and it takes all our strength—the grim-faced nurse's and mine—to heft him onto his hospital bed. Finally, Andrew lands on the mattress and blows out a stream of air. Catching his breath, he stares at the ceiling as if looking for leaks, then flaps his head toward us. "Thanks for the lift," he says. Then, "What am I, furniture?"

To my shock, the nurse smiles.

"I'll be right back with your IV," she says. "Don't go away."

Andrew snickers. "You caught me. I was planning my escape. JT made a rope out of pillowcases. I'm gonna climb out the window and shimmy down the building."

"I'll open the window for you," the nurse says on her way out, a smile stretched into a half-moon across her face.

"You got her," I say. "How do you do it? Unbelievable."

Andrew coughs. "She's crazy about me. When she was lifting me into the bed, she grabbed my ass." He coughs again, a louder, more insistent hack. He allows the cough to dissolve and then gently rubs his throat. "Unless that was you."

"That was me," I say, and then I picture Andrew squeezing through the hospital room window and lowering himself down the side of the hospital, hand over hand, gripping the rope of pillowcases. The image cracks me up.

"What?" he says, the word again becoming a cough.

"I just imagined you shimmying down the side of the building with pillowcases tied together."

"Yeah, well, when you're in the shit, brother, no matter how bad things seem, you gotta look for a way out."

The words stop me. He looks up at the ceiling again and says with quiet insistence, "There's always a way out, JT."

18.

The Fifth Session

"Listen"

Los Angeles
December 2007

WE SIT IN the doctor's office, the two of us, Andrew on an examination table, his head down, his feet dangling over the side. I sit on an ass-numbing straight-backed chair jammed against the wall by the door at the far end of the room, placed there like an afterthought. We sit in silence as the doctor, young, tall, runner's build, kind eyes beneath an expensive haircut, stares grim-faced at Andrew's chart. Other than "Hello, how are you feeling?" "Not bad, hanging in, how are you?" nobody has spoken. I feel momentarily transported back to high school, as if I've been banished to the principal's office or am in a classroom after school serving detention.

Eventually the doctor closes the chart and walks over to Andrew. The doctor places a hand on his hip and observes Andrew for a moment before he speaks. "You've been losing weight," he says.

"My lifelong dream," Andrew says.

The doctor snorts out a staccato laugh.

Andrew ticks names off on his fingers. "Weight Watchers, Jenny Craig, Atkins, the Zone. Nope. Nothing. I finally found something that works. Cancer."

"Well, ha, okay, but if possible, you have to try to eat more."

"It burns, man. Every time I swallow. Burns like hell. Makes it hard to eat. And believe me, I *love* to eat."

"I understand," the doctor says. "But even if you could do a little bit. Do the best you can. Have you tried Ensure?"

"That stuff tastes like Crisco. Hell, everything tastes like Crisco."

"What about water? We need you to stay hydrated."

Andrew sighs.

"Doing what you said last time," I say from across the room. "We pound a big bottle of water every day."

Andrew nods at me. "He's a taskmaster. He tells me, 'I'm not leaving until we finish this bottle.'"

The doctor follows Andrew's gaze in my direction. He seems to notice me for the first time. "That's good. Keep it up. Now." He sits on the edge of the examining table next to Andrew. "Let's go over the next step, where we are and where we're going."

"Okay. Listen up, JT."

"I got it."

Again the doctor looks at me, this time with something I take as suspicion.

"If I miss anything you say, JT's here," Andrew says. "I'm pretty good. I take notes, but JT's great. Good to have another set of ears."

I never considered listening to be a talent, but driving to chemo today Andrew called me a great listener. He said I had a gift.

"You've been listening intently your whole life. To your dad, whether you realized it or not, to the guys at DK when you were president, to sports talk when you became a caller, to callers, to your agents, to Julie if you're smart—"

"I even listen to you," I said.

"Sometimes," he said, grinning. "Yeah, you do. But today I need you to listen to the doctor."

"I'm on it," I said.

"Most people don't listen at all. They just want to hear themselves speak. Especially guys in our business."

"Well, it's called sports talk, not sports listen," I said.

"So you're the designated listener," the doctor says, squinting in my direction.

"I guess so, yeah."

"Smart to bring backup," the doctor says to Andrew, and then turns back to me. "You're his brother, right?"

I start to correct him.

"Yes," Andrew says quickly. "He's my brother."

19.

The Sixth Session

"More Importantly, How Are You Doing?"

Los Angeles
February 2008

THE TUMORS ARE SHRINKING.

But not quickly enough.

After an eight-week break, Andrew returns to City of Hope for his third round of chemotherapy.

He considers this a positive step.

When I pick him up for the first of four sessions over the next eight weeks, he practically bounds out of his house. He has lost more weight, but his cheeks look round and pink and he grins as I help him into the SUV.

"Yeah, babe," he says.

I circle around to the driver's side and climb behind the wheel. Andrew sits hunched over his BlackBerry, poking, texting, scrolling.

"I have to ask you a serious question," he says.

"Go for it."

"Last night. Why doesn't Kobe take the final shot? Why does he pass the ball away? What was he thinking?"

"Well, he was double-teamed—"

"So? Give me Kobe with two guys on him over Fisher standing all alone anytime. *Anytime.*"

And so it goes for the next ten minutes, Andrew and I conducting our own mini sports talk show in the front seat of my car. We passionately and loudly debate Kobe's decision making and shot selection, Phil Jackson's coaching style and philosophy, and which teams are likely to play for the NBA championship. When we've exhausted the subject of professional basketball, Andrew brings up another topic: my talk show.

"Heard you last night," he says, scrolling through e-mails on his smartphone. "You sounded good. Don't let up. Keep it going. Hey, when do the kids start T-ball? Opening day must be soon, right?"

On these rides, when we talk about sports or my kids or Andrew punches in the radio to listen to Fox, I know that he has slept well and has awakened feeling optimistic and energized, ready to kick this cancer's ass. "Bring it on," he'll say in the car if I ask how he feels.

Other times, on other rides, when he sits quietly, seemingly lost in thought, and he doesn't turn on the radio, I know he's feeling exhausted and beaten up.

"I had a rough night last night," he tells me on one drive, listlessly strapping his seat belt across his lap. "I'm not reacting well to the new meds. Got no sleep. Today is gonna be a major pain in the ass."

He goes quiet, closes his eyes, and dozes off for the rest of the ride.

Later, though, as he lies in his hospital bed receiving his ninth dose of chemo and the first of this new, highly aggressive mix, he perks up slightly and we talk sports. Andrew brings up the topic of pro athletes who've maintained long and successful careers. He respects longevity above all else. We talk about Mariano Rivera, Warren Moon, Grant Hill, and, of course, Brett Favre.

"These guys amaze me," he says. "Especially football players. They still get psyched up every Sunday and give it their all, everything they got, for *years*. Sometimes after a game or when they wake up Monday, they can't even *walk*. Can you imagine? It's unbelievable."

"Takes a certain kind of guy," I say. "They just keep going."

"At a high level," Andrew reminds me. "They perform for years at a very high level."

He turns his head toward me. His eyelids look dark and heavy.

"I was thinking about something," he says. He swallows, grimaces. "Pretty soon you're gonna be on the radio longer than *anybody* because of the double shift you did. We gotta figure out a way to remind people that nobody does more hours than you do. Nobody."

"Well, yeah, maybe, but that's not important. You should rest—"

He forces himself almost to a sitting position and steamrolls over everything I've said. "You're on longer than everyone, JT. Eventually people are gonna notice this. Do the math. Five nights a week, five hours a night. That's more than almost anybody. We have to make people aware of this. You need something, some PR or something. We gotta get something out of this."

He narrows his eyes. His face suddenly looks very drawn. "You must be so tired," he says.

"Me? No, man. I'm not tired. I'm fine—"

"I don't know how you do it. You come here with me, then you go back home, hang with the kids and Julie, then you go into work, do your show, and then you're back here with me. You have this crazy energy. How do you fucking do it?"

I shrug uncomfortably. "I'm a grinder."

"You're an iron man."

I shift uneasily in my chair. I want to shoot out of my seat and pace through the room, but I anchor my feet and lean forward in my chair.

"Andrew, why are you bringing this up? You're fighting for your life. What you're going through is much harder—"

He cuts me off. "I go here and I go home. You're the one with the insane hours. I don't do anything. Shit, I don't even drive."

"You're right," I say. "You got it easy. I got it rough."

He cracks up, his laugh morphing into a cough. He lies back down, fighting to find a comfortable spot. "Just thinking about your hours, I get tired."

"Yeah, that must be what's knocking you out."

"Warren Moon, babe. Guy played until he was like fifty. That's you. The Warren Moon of radio."

He sighs again and closes his eyes. Within minutes, the chemo coursing through him, he falls into a deep, noisy sleep.

Jeff McCarthy, Andrew's former boss who fired him but has remained a close friend, told me, "If you asked Andrew how he was doing, he would say, 'More importantly, how are *you* doing?' He means it. That's who he is and why people love him. He cares more about you than himself."

A few days after driving Andrew for this round of chemo, Matt and Lisa, my agents, call me.

"Andrew contacted us," Lisa says.

"He wants to talk about a contract extension," Matt says.

"He wants to make sure you're okay," Lisa says.

"He wants to make sure *I'm* okay?"

"I know," Matt says. "What's wrong with this picture?"

"He says you got a lot on your plate," Lisa says.

"He doesn't want you to worry about anything," Matt says.

"That's Andrew," Lisa says.

The contract negotiations occur quickly and bloodlessly, and when Matt and Lisa lock down the language, Fox Radio sends out a press release announcing that I have been extended for two more years.

Andrew feels more exhausted than usual for his next chemo session so I meet him at his front door and walk him to the car, steering him by the elbow.

"By the way, congratulations," he says.

"Thank you," I say. "And I mean, thank *you*."

Andrew grunts. "You deserve it. So, good, it looks like you're gonna be around for a while."

"You, too," I say. "You will be, too."

He exhales and doesn't answer.

20.

The Seventh Session

"Don't Back Down"

Los Angeles–Glendale, Arizona
February 2008

AFTER CHEMO TODAY, Andrew doesn't feel up to walking through the parking lot to the car. We exit the main building and I sit him at the bench by the curb. I jog into the lot, find my car, hop in, and pull up next to him. I help Andrew into the passenger seat and then swing around to the driver's side. Except for the occasional tapping of my fingers on the steering wheel, silence fills the car. I wait for Andrew to reach over and turn on the radio, but he keeps his hands folded in his lap.

Usually on the drive to City of Hope, Andrew astonishes me with his energy and positive attitude. On the way back, though, he will sit silently for the first few minutes. He seems to go off into his own world, lost in thought, gathering strength, calming himself, or maybe even meditating. I'm not sure. We never talk about it. Then, at some point, he will reach for the radio. I don't say anything, but that tiny movement of his finger pressing the tuner button fills me with relief and even hope. *The chemo is working*, I think. *We are winning.*

But the last couple of times when we left City of Hope, the silence in the car hung dark and heavy. Andrew said nothing at all during the entire return trip unless I spoke to him and asked a direct question. And he never turned on the radio.

It's getting to him. How can it not?

Today I feel the silence filling the front seat like a thick cloud. I'm sure he's worn down from the hours he's just spent lying with an IV in his arm and perhaps more from anticipating the days of sickness ahead. He never talks about what he goes through at home, but I've known he experiences a kind of hell. I've read and heard about the nausea, vomiting, diarrhea, fever, dizziness, overall excruciating soreness, and debilitating exhaustion. In the quiet of the car on our drives to and from City of Hope I see the best of him.

I now understand at least one reason why Andrew asked me to be his chemotherapy partner. Sandra, his new wife, took her marriage vows to stand by him in sickness and in health less than a year ago. And this she does, especially as he recovers from each chemo session, caring for him at home, all day, every day. By stepping in and taking Andrew to chemotherapy and occasional doctor's appointments, I'm able to give her something of a break.

I can't imagine how Sandra must feel, watching her role in Andrew's life change so radically over only a few months, going from newlywed to nurse. I know that Andrew's battle with cancer is devastating for her, too.

I think of all Andrew has done for me, from mailing me his playbook, to offering me advice, to serving as my sounding board, to hosting me at his home, to being my champion and mentor in life and on the radio. And I think, *Yes, I want to do everything I can for Andrew... and for Sandra.*

It's what friends do.

———

I won't back down.

February 3, 2008.

Super Bowl XLII.

A heavy underdog, the New York Giants, my team, roll into Glendale, Arizona, to take on the undefeated and supposedly invincible New England Patriots. Ultimately, the Giants will pull off a huge upset, 17–14, executing an 83-yard touchdown drive with two minutes left, in what some call the greatest comeback in Super Bowl history.

Andrew and I watch the game sitting side by side on a couch in the Fox Radio executive suite at University of Phoenix Stadium.

With the Patriots leading 7–3 at the half, I swing off the couch, step over to the bar, and return with two bottles of water. I twist both tops off and hand a bottle to Andrew.

"We're pounding these," I say, doctor's orders ringing in my head, urging Andrew on. He takes a couple of weak, painful sips, sets the bottle down next to him. "That's all I can do," he says.

"All right, good job, you'll take some more later." I smile at him and we fist bump.

We settle back against the wall of pillows we've propped behind us. For much of the first half, Fox employees have paid quick visits to Andrew, joking with him, trying to engage him. Andrew smiles, laughs on occasion, but for the most part he keeps unusually quiet, a thoughtful look on his face, observing the swirl of activity around him. Now, on the field and on the monitor in front of us, the cameras focus on Tom Petty and the Heartbreakers, who begin the halftime show, charging through a rousing version of "American Girl." The stadium crowd erupts in applause and then Tom Petty slides right into "I Won't Back Down."

"Yeah, babe." Andrew laughs, bites his lip in typical white guy dance mode, bobs his head to the music, then sings along to lyrics Tom Petty could have written for him personally: *"You can stand me up at the gates of hell and I won't back down."*

I join him for the chorus, howling, *"I won't back down..."*

And then I remember...

The AFC Championship Game in Oakland.

Five years earlier.

Julie and I, married four months, live in our tiny apartment, not remotely big enough for the two of us, a joke when Andrew crashes on our couch the night before the game. Between his plus-size body and mammoth personality, Andrew pretty much overwhelms every room he enters. He *demolishes* our apartment. We laugh about it.

"Next time I'm staying in a hotel," he says.

"What? Why?" I say. "We got plenty of room."

"Fine," Julie says. "*I'll* stay in a hotel."

I kiss Julie, hug Andrew, and head to the stadium for the Raiders pregame show.

An hour or so later, Julie and Andrew start over to Oakland in Julie's finicky bright pink Chevy Blazer we call the Barbie Blazer. After a torturously stop-and-go ride in bumper-to-bumper traffic, they turn into the stadium's parking lot, which looks like a scene from one of the *Mad Max* movies—heavy metal music screaming a head-thumping soundtrack; the smell of burning flesh accompanied by black smoke billowing from fires raging in barbecue pits; and thousands of bikers, gang-bangers, and variations of straight-out scary people in costume massing throughout the parking lot, descending randomly on entering cars.

"End of the world," Andrew says, peering through the windshield.

"Or, as we call it, a Raiders home game."

Julie inches the Barbie Blazer forward and stops, pressed up to the car in front of her.

"This ain't happening," Andrew says. "Pull over to the side."

He points to a couple of cops looking helpless and on edge.

Julie eases the car away from the stream of traffic toward the cops as Andrew rolls down his window. "Officers! I got JT the Brick's wife. He's on the air. We need to get to the stadium."

The cops jump into action and begin directing traffic, halting a line of cars, clearing a path, and waving the Barbie Blazer through.

The Blazer blows past the cops, moves a hundred feet forward, and then dies.

"I don't believe this," Julie says.

"Are you out of gas?"

"It won't turn over. It's dead."

Andrew slams open the passenger door and starts to step out.

"Where you going?"

Channeling his most nasally Tom Petty, Andrew belts, *"Oh, no, I won't back down."* He gets into a wrestler's crouch behind the Blazer, grips the bumper, and cranes his neck to the side so Julie can see him. "Put it in neutral and steer!"

"Okay..."

"Ready? Go!"

Andrew lowers his shoulder and shoves.

The Blazer doesn't budge.

Red-faced, gritting his teeth, Andrew stands, then lowers his body again and puts all of his 300-plus pounds into the back of the Blazer.

The Blazer rolls forward a foot.

Andrew, his face now pulsing an alarming shade of purple, grunts, groans, doesn't give in, doesn't stop. He sucks down a breath, exhales, growls like a bear, and keeps pushing.

The Blazer picks up speed.

The sea of humanity in front parts and the Blazer, with this mountain of a guy in a leather jacket crouched and pushing the car forward, his face flushed, purple as a grape, sweat streaming down it, arrives at a spot near the entrance of the stadium, close enough for Julie and Andrew to make a run for it.

"You okay?" Julie calls to Andrew.

Andrew grunts in her direction and waves a hand blackened by grease or tire soot, swipes at the sweat pooling on his forehead, leaving a black streak, and stammers, "Gotta... catch... my... breath."

Julie nods at the Blazer. "Should I just leave it here? It'll get stripped."

"Would be…an…improvement."

Julie and Andrew find me inside the stadium a minute before kickoff. "I kept calling," I say. "What the hell happened? You're a mess, dude."

"Thank you. Tell you all about it later."

Keep this world from dragging me down.

And now, my memory jogged, a smile stitched across my face, I look at Andrew stretched out next to me on the couch in the Fox suite. He catches my eye and turns away from Tom Petty. "What?"

"I was just thinking about the time you pushed the Blazer through the parking lot in Oakland."

"Shit. That was crazy."

"You must've really felt like you could've been messed up."

"Oh, yeah. But you know me—"

And Andrew Ashwood, formerly BJ Hunter, radio jock, once the king of morning drive, the master of cueing up a song and talking right up to the exact moment the vocal starts, finishes singing along with Tom Petty live at halftime of the Super Bowl, *"Nooo, I won't back down."*

21.

The Eighth Session

"Don't Stress, Don't Obsess, Be a Mentor"

Los Angeles
March 2008

IN THE COURSE of one week, I take Andrew to chemotherapy and radiation treatments four times. Each time I pick him up at his house he says good-bye to Sandra and greets me the same way, "Yeah, babe. Let's go." And each time he moves slower and speaks softer, but he says these four words with more conviction than I have yet heard. Awash in this attitude, never expressing anything less than a completely positive attitude, his e-mails to friends and family often end with what has become his signature: "WINNING is my only option."

As he receives his latest dose of chemo, our laptops flipped open, the day's newspapers strewn all over—on his bed, across two chairs, atop the movable table at his side, spread on the floor—he speaks rarely and, when he does, quietly and with reflection. When he finally finds the strength to begin a conversation, he talks urgently, as if he can concentrate for only a few seconds.

"You're in a good position," he says suddenly. "I'm a chess player so I try to think a couple of moves ahead."

He swallows, waits for me to respond.

"Right," I say.

"You always want to be on at night."

I slide to the edge of my chair, getting closer so he doesn't have to raise his voice. I have a history of badgering Andrew about my time slot—among other issues—always wondering if anyone knows I even exist. Often I have lobbied hard to my agents and Andrew about switching from nights to afternoon or morning drive.

"Why is being on at night a good thing?" I ask Andrew.

"Because you're on great radio stations. The best ones in the country. And people listen longer at night. Program directors will hear you, I promise. That's how *I* heard you."

"The playbook," I say.

Andrew smiles. "That's right. I sent that to a few people. Nobody responded the way you did."

"Well, the way you put everything together was unbelievable. It was invaluable."

"That's another thing." He turns to me. His forehead creases. I can tell he is in pain. He doesn't go there. He starts to gesture, stops, realizes his movements are restricted by the IV attached to his arm. "Always appreciate your people. Reach out to them. Write a letter. A handwritten letter. Mail it to them. Snail mail. Not e-mail."

"A thank-you note."

"Goes a long way." He holds for a moment, and then through a torrent of breath, he rattles off, in rapid fire, a list of lessons. "Don't stress out. Don't get divorced. Live the right way. Have a strong family."

"Stress out? *Me?*"

A garbled noise, which I recognize as a laugh, escapes from his throat. "Gonna ignore that. Oh. Do not e-mail your boss, or anyone, when you're emotional. Sleep on it. Chill. Don't burn bridges. Don't *obsess.*"

"I'm working on that one."

"Finally, be a mentor. Help someone out. Pass on what you've learned. *Give.* Don't take. GIVE. It's good for your soul. And with a mentor—"

He can't finish the rest of the sentence. He swallows again, then rubs this throat. He closes his eyes and turns his head toward the wall. He speaks quietly. I strain to hear his words.

"—you always have someone to talk to."

22.

The Ninth Session

"Good Luck, Good Life, Good Love"

Los Angeles–Tampa, Florida
August–September 2008

TIME FLICKS BY. At the end of the summer, Andrew sends a mass e-mail to everyone at Fox updating his health status. In the subject line he writes: "SHRINKAGE is a Good Thing!"

He says he's sorry he's been absent for a while and then provides a long, detailed medical update. He explains that recent scans have shown the original tumors have shrunk, but the cancer has spread into his lymph nodes. He calls this "a couple new areas of concern." He praises the City of Hope doctors who jumped in immediately and attacked this unforeseen advance into his nodes with a new mix of chemicals. "The new mix IS working," Andrew writes, and says that he will resume treatments beginning Monday, August 25—his *fifth* round of chemotherapy. His optimism remains unshakable.

"This bastard is tough," he writes, "but we are tougher and

have no intention of giving in and plan on making that transition from fighter to survivor, sooner or later."

He thanks everyone for their incredible support. His only real regret is how much he misses being in the office every day. He signs off, proclaiming as always, "WINNING is MY only option."

I e-mail him back. I tell that he has fought like a "MOTHERFUCKIN CHAMP." I say that he has never gotten soft and to always keep victory in his sights. I urge him to "keep fighting and we will win," and I tell him that I love him.

He writes me back, saying, simply, "Amen, my brother!" He ends this brief e-mail with: "Chemo tomorrow. Bring it on!"

———

At chemo, after he flirts with the middle-aged nurse who attaches his IV and shakes her head and closes the door on her way out, I tell Andrew how much his e-mail meant to everyone at Fox. Several people have contacted me offering Andrew their support and sending good wishes as he enters his next phase of chemotherapy.

"I have to admit, after that last round I thought they would be able to operate," he says. "We're not there yet."

He rustles in the bed, clears his throat, and twists around in the sheets, trying to get comfortable. He face looks drawn and pale and his eyes have gone cloudy. It strikes me now that even though I've often seen him when he was physically weak and exhausted, this is the first time I've ever detected a note of real concern, something that even approaches defeat. He sighs. "Nope. Not there," he says again.

"Okay," I say.

"Getting there, though. Yeah, getting there. Staying positive."

"That's why you're gonna win. That attitude. That energy."

"Well," Andrew says. "You know, I'm—"

He swallows and jams his eyes closed. His eyelids flutter as if he's trying to ward off a sudden wave of pain. He frowns, opens his eyes, blinks, and then slaps the bed with his off hand, the one not attached to the IV. "I'm down to third and long here, JT. We're not at fourth down yet, but—"

"You gotta keep fighting, man. The chemo is working. You said so yourself. The new mix of chemicals is *working*. It's not third down. It's *first* down. First and goal. We're driving. We're gonna get to the house. We gotta keep fighting."

Andrew reaches over and takes my hand. "You're right. It's first down. Hell, it's a whole new ball game. We're gonna win. We have to."

"Our only option," I say.

He nods and drops his head onto the pillow.

I hold his hand until he falls asleep.

———

He sleeps most of the way home. When we pull into his driveway, I call his name twice. He doesn't respond. I gently nudge him awake. His eyes fly open and for a moment he looks at me blankly as if he doesn't know me. He finally nods with recognition and struggles to sit up in his seat. I run over to the passenger side of the SUV and help him out. Slowly, we walk to his front door. He steps heavily, his Ugg boots making a soft, squishy sound. At one point, he shivers.

"I'm cold," he says.

It's August, I think.

The words scream at me.

We reach the front door and I help him inside.

"Thanks, JT," he says. "Sorry. I'm a little out of it today."

"You did great today, man, *great*. I'll see you tomorrow."

I rush back to the SUV and climb behind the wheel. I jerk the car into reverse, roar down his tiny driveway as if it's a drag strip, slam the car into drive, and rocket toward the end of his street, rows of rush hour traffic just behind me on the freeway thrumming in white noise. And then I slam on the brakes, pull over to the curb, and stop. I peer through the windshield for a few seconds and then I bury my head in my hands and I pray. "Please," I say. "Please let him be okay. Please let him make it. Please."

The sobs come then, careening through me. I drop my head onto the steering wheel and I let the crying come harder, faster, and then, finally, after ten or fifteen minutes, I have no idea how long, I slowly lift my head, wipe my eyes and my nose with the bottom of my shirt, exhale from the depths of my diaphragm, and drive home to my wife and kids.

—

I get a call from Bruce Allen.

Bruce, former special assistant to Al Davis and the Oakland Raiders and previously my boss, has taken over as general manager of the Tampa Bay Buccaneers. According to Andrew, Bruce lives in the most exclusive section of the area, rubbing shoulders with the likes of Mariano Rivera.

As I speak with Bruce I scan through my NFL schedule and find what I'm looking for: the Packers will be playing the Bucs September 25. I write the date on a legal pad and circle the numbers ferociously. "I've been thinking we need to arrange a road trip for Andrew," I say.

"How soon?"

"Soon."

"You're talking about the Packers game, right?"

"Any chance?"

"Done. I'll make it happen."

Only a few of us make this trip with Andrew—Sandra, Jeff, Dresch, Timm Amundson, his good friend Gabe Hobbs, Jimmy B., and me. Bruce arranges everything, covering every detail from travel, transportation and accommodations to dinner and tickets to the game.

The night before the game, we gather around the dinner table, eight people, all of us friends, most of us connected by Andrew. He is our hub, the glue of this group, as he is for so many other people across so many other groups. Recently, sitting with him at chemotherapy, I tried to create a "friendship circle," putting Andrew at the center, writing down the names of all the people he connected. I gave up after a few minutes. There were simply too many people to list.

I look over at him, sitting at the head of the table. Ten months after our trip to Green Bay, I gauge how much he's changed. He appears gaunt and weak. His shirt, a favorite of his, once blousy and oversize to conceal his 300-pound frame, now hangs off him. He smiles often, but his eyes, which to me always carried a mischievous twinkle, now seem sad and heavy-lidded. He seems to hold a faraway look that suggests he's either observing or slightly disoriented. What bothers me most, though, is that when we hug, his arms wrap around me weakly, thin as twigs.

We offer toasts and tell stories. Jeff celebrates Andrew's sense of adventure and recounts their epic trip to Germany nearly nineteen years earlier when, as young members of the media, they witnessed the fall of the Berlin Wall, running through the insane crowds and racing from checkpoint to checkpoint in a tiny foreign car. The rest of us follow with loving, emotional words of encouragement, echoing Andrew's favorite themes, "Winning is my only option" and "Dare to be great."

And then Andrew slowly rises to his feet. Someone clinks a knife against a glass. The room goes quiet.

"I want to make a toast," Andrew says, lifting his water glass. "To all of you here, my inner circle, thank you. Now, okay. I want you all to wipe away any sadness. I'm in this fight and I have great support and I'm gonna win this thing, but if I don't—"

He stops to swallow and catch his breath. He measures his words.

"If I *don't*...I want you to have a big fucking party. My whole life was a party, every minute, and I want you to keep it going. No tears, no sad speeches, none of that. You can stop for a minute and toast me, but then get back to it. Keep it raging. *Party*. That's what I want. Those are my wishes."

We stand, raise our glasses, and toast Andrew. I glance around the room and see that most of us, at once, are fighting back tears. I take my seat, and as I pour myself another drink, I think of Andrew as BJ Hunter, morning-drive disc jockey. He would end every show with a catchphrase: "Good luck, good life, good love." I decide to raise my glass to Andrew and offer that sentiment to the room, but he has moved away from the table and is sitting in the corner in an intimate conversation with Bruce. Andrew listens intently, his eyes wide, animated, as Bruce speaks to him. Finally, Andrew nods and then they throw their arms around each other.

I don't know for sure, but I believe that Bruce and Andrew have said good-bye.

Good luck, good life, good love.

23.

The Tenth Session

"Learn to Say Good-bye"

Los Angeles
October–November 2008

WHEN WE GET back from Tampa, I call Greg Papa, the play-by-play announcer of the Oakland Raiders, a friend of mine and an old buddy of Andrew's.

"How's he doing?" Papa asks me.

I pause and feel my voice catch in my throat. "I think you might want to come down here and see him."

A week later, I pick up Papa at the Los Angeles Airport and drive him to Andrew's house. I escort Greg to the front door. We ring the bell and wait while Andrew shuffles down the hall in his Uggs. When Greg and Andrew see each other, they embrace, and then Andrew leads Greg inside. I close the front door behind them and head back to my car to run errands. When I return two hours later and ring Andrew's doorbell, Andrew and Greg come to the door together. They open the front door and hug in the doorway. Greg breaks away and I see that his eyes are red and his cheeks are moist.

"Thanks for connecting me with Andrew, JT," Greg says in the car as we head over the hill from the San Fernando Valley toward his hotel by the airport. "It meant a lot."

"For me, too," I say.

The next Sunday, lying next to each other on his bed, Andrew and I watch the Packers. Each chemo session now seems to take a greater toll. Andrew has spent this entire week recovering and still he feels exhausted. His beloved Packers seem to momentarily rejuvenate him. He finds the strength to cheer, to complain about the officiating, to question the play calling, to rail at dropped receptions and missed tackles. At halftime, he sips water, chews ice chips, and regroups, psyching himself up for the second half.

"I'm thinking about going to Toohey's wedding," he says, quietly.

"Wow. Excellent."

"Sandra and Julie have worked out the details. The four of us would go together. You're driving."

"I knew *I* was going. I'm glad you're thinking about it."

"It'll be a game-time decision," Andrew says. He pauses. "I want to say good-bye. Well, I'm not actually gonna *say* good-bye..."

"Come on—"

Andrew raises his hand, giving me the stop sign.

"Knowing when to say good-bye is not a bad thing," he says. "You know the guy at the party who doesn't know when to leave? He just hangs around like a jerk after everyone else has gone, but you don't want to be rude and tell him, 'Hey, dude, the party's over, go home.'"

"Always one at every party," I say. "Clueless."

"I don't want to be that guy," Andrew says.

"You're never that guy. You *are* the party."

"Yeah, well, you have to learn to work the room, JT. That's real important. You got that down."

"I was always pretty good, but then I got to watch you in action. You take working the room to another level. I'm still learning from you."

"You also have to know when to shut it down, when it's time to go." He sips some water, swallows painfully. "You gotta learn when to say good-bye."

Andrew gives himself the go-ahead.

The following Saturday the four of us drive over an hour to the wedding of Greg Toohey, a friend and Fox employee, held at a country club in a beautiful spot in the middle of nowhere. Andrew, riding shotgun, doesn't say much. At one point he shifts in his seat uncomfortably, noisily, follows that up with a mighty sigh, and I wonder if he's made the wrong decision. Soon, though, we locate the country club, park near the entrance, and Andrew pulls himself out of the car, inhales, and catches a second—or first—wind. As I've seen so many times in the past thirteen months, he appears to turn on an internal switch that somehow allows him to retrieve an extra boost of energy. As we watch the ceremony and then locate our table for the reception, Andrew, although he's quieter than usual and an observer more than a participant, seems almost himself. He laughs, engages with everyone, and perks up whenever anyone approaches. At one point, Sandra, Andrew, Julie, and I cram into the portable photo booth in the corner of the reception hall and pose for a strip of pictures. The women go for the sexy Bond girl look and Andrew and I clown around, spread our arms wide, and make ridiculous, goofy faces. Scrunched together in this tiny booth behind the flimsy, rickety curtain, we lose it, the four of us, dissolving into uncontrollable laughter. We return to our table and Julie carefully places our copy of the photos in her purse, as if these pictures are a cherished keepsake.

As the reception winds down, while I stand at the bar ordering a last round of drinks, I catch Andrew speaking with Dave Coelho, a former Fox employee, *former* because Andrew fired him. Dave is a close friend and I know Andrew's firing hit him hard. I knew Dave would be here and I wondered how he and Andrew would react when they saw each other. Now, out of earshot, I watch them talking intensely for several minutes, both of them nodding, and then laughing, and then they hug.

After we make a final toast to the bride and groom and start to head out, more than one person takes me aside and says, "He seems to be doing pretty well." I have to agree. I know that this last round of chemo has kicked his ass, but as we get back into the car and settle in for the long ride home and I watch Andrew drift off to sleep against the passenger door, I feel that maybe he's started to turn a corner.

———

November 10, 2008.

Sherman Oaks, California.

I'm outside. Standing on a ladder. Painting the back porch with my dad. He and my mom are out from New York. My dad can't sit still. When my parents visit, Julie and the kids regularly hit the mall with Grandma. As for Dad, I find stuff around the house for him to fix, rewire, patch, or paint. He lives for DIY. He demands a list. This I provide.

A sharp, cool breeze bites my face. I flick at the wind as if it's a pesky insect. Brush it off. The sting of the cool doesn't faze me or my dad. We're New Yorkers. Diehards. We defy the weather with cargo shorts and paint-spattered T-shirts.

I suck at puttering around the house. I hand over all home repairs to Julie. My idea of fixing something is whacking it with a hammer—screwing it up worse—then calling our shady handyman, who gets it done, charging golden time. But when my dad arrives, I jump in with him. Male bonding. Guys doing guy stuff. I dig in, climb up a ladder, slather on paint with a roller, pretending I have a clue, longing for a beverage break. As I said, when it comes to working with my hands, I got no game. My dad doesn't care. He just likes seeing me put in the effort and knows I'm doing it for him.

Plus, two guys outside slapping on a second coat, we talk sports and money. A combustible combination. The conservative accountant in him rails against owners paying big stars obscene franchise-busting salaries. *Twenty-five mil a year for A-Rod? Are you kidding me? Joe D., the Yankee Clipper, the greatest Yankee ever, held out for a HUNDRED GRAND.* My dad, great former jock and still athletic in his late seventies, springs out of a crouch and waves his brush up at me. *Freakin' A-Rod makes more than that per GAME.*

I laugh. Dad's got a point. I half consider putting him on the radio with me tonight. I watch his mind click, whir, crunch the numbers.

"He makes thirty-seven five per at bat," he says.

"That's like ten grand per swing," I say.

We're both laughing now. Losing it. Paint dripping onto the browning November lawn.

We're laughing so hard we don't hear the phone ring.

Twenty minutes later, my dad cleaning the brushes over a bucket with a rag, I bang into the kitchen and pour us a couple of tall ice teas from a pitcher Julie left on the counter. I reach for my cell and find my voice mail glaring bloodred. I punch it.

Sandra.

I slam the phone to my ear.

"JT, pick up, it's Andrew." Her voice stabs me. "JT, it's *Andrew*. You there? JT? He stopped breathing. The ambulance is here."

My hands shaking, I call her back. She answers before I hear a ring. Her voice sounds distant, lost. "JT."

"Sandra, which hospital?"

She tells me. Ten minutes from my house. I know the place. Across from the park where my kids play Little League.

"Dad," I say. I'm flying across the lawn, one arm shoved into the sleeve of my jacket, the other flapping in the breeze. "It's Andrew."

My dad slides the paintbrushes into the bucket. His eyes darken and he whispers into the grass. "Call me."

I roll behind the wheel of the SUV, my adrenaline pumping, wired as a getaway driver. I kick into reverse, bomb backward down the driveway, roar up the street. I hit a red light on Woodman at the freeway entrance. I pound the steering wheel with my palm.

"Come *on*," I say, pissed at the traffic, pissed at the world. I swallow, and a sour taste tumbles up from my stomach into my throat.

The red light goes green and I pass a car—stupid—practically force him off the ramp, and hit the 101, a maniac, barreling by and weaving through cars, fingers white on the wheel, Steve McQueen in *Bullitt*.

The anger boils off and I feel numb.

Then I hear his voice like he's sitting next to me.

We're gonna beat this, JT.

A tear snakes down my cheek.

"Please, Andrew," I say. "Not yet."

I pull into the hospital parking lot.

Hoping to hell that I'm not too late.

I am.

Too late.

Sandra is sitting on the edge of a chair outside the ER. She's slumped over, her head in her hands. I sit down next to her. She raises her head. Her face is so wet it looks as if she's been swimming.

"He's in a coma," she says. "He had a massive heart attack."

All I can do is nod.

I lose my sense of time. Doctors in scrubs passing by, nurses on the move, EMTs wheeling patients, family and friends following, their faces cemented in ghostlike masks. The twin ER doors whap open, swing shut like saloon doors in an old Western. Thirty minutes later, an hour—I can't tell—a doctor in dirty green materializes, pulls up a chair, and sits across from us. Words float by: *unconscious, intensive care, organs shut down, matter of days, funeral arrangements, loose ends, so, so, so sorry.* He and Sandra stand at the same time. It almost looks as if he's about to shake her hand and thank her for coming, but he walks her through the saloon doors. The doors whistle, flutter, close. Footsteps echo, fade. My head throbs. My legs feel rubbery. I don't dare move. After several minutes, a nurse appears. I straighten up as she speaks. She murmurs something I don't catch. I feel myself rise. She shoves her shoulder into the double doors.

I trail her. A right, a left. ICU. The temperature plummets, followed by an eerie quiet, as if someone has turned down the sound. Low voices. Tiny clicks, clacks, whirring. The nurse stops and gestures toward a room as if she's on a game show showing me what I won. I enter the room.

Andrew lies in a bed, tubes and wires everywhere. Blocky black machines jut up against him, groaning like Darth Vader's breathing. Andrew's eyes are closed and swollen. His face looks purple and peaceful and sad.

I feel my pulse race.

I know that I will never speak to him again.

I stagger as if I've been blinded and lower myself into a chair.

Andrew.

We said, often, that we loved each other.

I haven't yet said that to my parents.

Yes, I love you. Everybody loves you. And you love everyone. You make every single person feel like your best friend.

I love you.

Andrew.

I never got to say thank you.

You came into my life like a big wide tornado, lifted me up, shook me, and put me down in a better place.

Without you, I never meet my wife. Never meet Julie. Never have my kids.

I never have my career.

I never become the man I am. I never become the father, the son, the husband, the friend I am. I will always be a work in progress. We know that. But without you, I don't do the work and I don't progress. You got me to focus on what mattered.

You made me see.

So many things.

The importance of staying close. Bringing people in.

Connection.

Friendship.

We both value our friends so much.

Man love.

You showed me how to embrace that.

Andrew, you taught me by doing. You showed me.

Grab life by the throat. Make every day a party. Savor each moment. Hug. Yes, hug. And keep fighting. Never give up. Kick that cancer bastard in the balls. Fight. Keep fighting. Fight like each day is your...last.

You showed me how to live, Andrew.

And then...you showed me how to die.

I swipe my nose with the back of my hand.

My chest heaves. I feel my whole body shake. I'm trembling.

Andrew.

Thank you.

For everything.

And...good-bye.

Andrew passes away a few days later in his hospital room. In the days that follow, I do my best to support Sandra and help with the arrangements for Andrew's memorial service. I speak with Michael Drescher and Jeff Rowe, two of Andrew's dearest friends, about the reception after the service.

"He didn't want us to grieve," I say.

"He wanted a party," Jeff says. "A big blowout celebration."

"At my house, too," Dresch says. "I'm on it."

After the memorial service at Forest Lawn Cemetery, we caravan, a fleet of cars filled with Andrew's friends and family. We drive across Sunset Boulevard and up into the Doheny Hills to Dresch's multilevel contemporary overlooking the expanse of

Los Angeles all the way to the Pacific. Stepping to the front door alone with Julie, the caravan dispersed or lost, I hear the rumble of a familiar AC/DC bass line blasting from inside Dresch's house.

"Tearing down the walls," I say. "Just the way he wanted."

We enter the house and step down into a sunken living room. We stop, freeze in our tracks.

Facing us on the mantel is a color photo of Andrew, blown up beyond poster size, his face pink and full and healthy and stretched into a wide smile, his long blond hair blowing in some breeze, the strands tickling the shoulders of his billowing white shirt. He appears, of course, larger than life, as he always did. But now, in this soft L.A. afternoon light, he looks like a beautiful, grinning, peaceful, oversize angel.

We take him in, take in that *peace*, and then drift through the living room up a few stairs and find drinks and food. We fill glasses and plates and exchange hellos and nods and hugs, and then more people arrive, a few at first and then a steady stream, and the noise level rises and we share stories and we laugh, and we choke up, and before we know it night falls, and the party heats up and someone turns the music up and the bass line throbs through me, hollows me out, people holler above it, and more mournful crying comes and louder laughter, hysterics, and I toast glass after glass with family and down shots with friends and strangers and the party morphs into the kind of semi-out-of-control rager I shared so many times with Andrew, in San Antonio, at Final Fours, at Super Bowls, at Daytona. This one hits a crescendo, becoming a party for all time, melding into one last giant blowout, with Andrew grinning over us, seeming to oversee his very own send-off. When finally we head for the door, Julie's arm linked through mine, my head throbbing more from exhaustion and loss than from alcohol, we stagger wordlessly out of Dresch's house and onto his driveway, squinting into an orange flare, what I realize is the dawn breaking.

I spend the next few weeks in a kind of trance, moving through my days slowly, my legs heavy, as if I'm traveling through mud. I try to lose myself in work and succeed to some extent, but I find myself veering away from people, not wanting to say much. At night, after my show, when my head hits the pillow I'm unable to fall asleep. I find myself staring into the dark, into nothing-ness, my body aching with loneliness.

One afternoon, the doorbell rings. I open the front door to find Sandra standing outside holding a folded-over grocery bag.

"How you doing?" I say.

She shrugs. I nod. I point my thumb toward my living room. "Come on in."

"No, I can't stay. I just..." She lowers her eyes to the ground, then raises her head and a tiny smile appears. "I've been going through his... stuff. Julie's been helping."

"Yeah, she's been telling me. It must be tough."

"There's a lot." She exhales, then looks at the bag as if notic-ing it for the first time. "I thought..." She pauses, straightens her back, gathers some strength. "I wanted you to have these. I think Andrew would've liked that."

She extends the bag toward my chest. I clutch it, look back at Sandra. "Thanks. You sure you don't want to come in—"

"No, I'm going to go."

She flutters her hand in front of her face as her eyes fill with tears.

Before I can say anything else, she turns and walks toward her car. I watch her drive off and then I edge back into the living room. I close the door, hesitate, and reach into the bag.

I pull out Andrew's Uggs boots.

I feel a tug in my throat. I look at the boots, feel their weight in my hands, and then place them on the floor in front of me. For several moments I just stare at them.

Then I carry the boots to the couch. I sit at the edge of the cushion and yank off my shoes. I take a deep breath and slip on Andrew's boots. My socks sink into the soft, warm fur lining.

I stand up and slowly walk across the living room, taking small, tentative steps. I picture him in the boots, remembering how he wore them almost every day to fight off the cold, even in summer. I look at the boots as I walk across the room and I feel an emotion that carries me beyond my sadness and loneliness and grief.

I'm walking in his shoes, I think. *I'm walking in Andrew's shoes.*

I feel something that approaches...pride.

I wear his boots to this day.

24.

Swimming in the Desert

Las Vegas
Today

I ALWAYS KNEW I'd end up in Vegas. The truth is even though Jimmy Baxter and I embarked on that epic trip—our escape from New York—nearly twenty-five years ago, hell-bent for San Diego, at heart I never felt like a California guy. I wanted the weather; I dreamed about living in a place where I could wear a T-shirt and shorts 24/7. After enduring twenty-plus brutal freezing East Coast winters, I craved the heat. All signs pointed to California. But the moment I got a taste of the desert and the never-ending insanity and excitement pulsing like a live wire down the Las Vegas Strip, I fell in love. Or at least I got hooked. And once I met Julie and learned that she felt the same way, I knew I'd found my home.

After Andrew passed, I made it my goal to get back to Las Vegas. I know that Vegas is not to everyone's taste and some people might think I'm crazy to say this, but I believe that Las Vegas is a great place to raise a family. A few miles outside the center of Sin City, away from the high rollers, high-end hook-ers, and wild partying, you find suburbs that in a weird way remind me of Long Island, where I grew up, suburbs with good schools in safe, quiet communities composed of hardworking, like-minded people. Maybe it's a stretch, but I see some of Massapequa in the middle of the Nevada desert.

Anyway, here I am, living in a house that would have blown An-drew's mind. Blew my mom's and dad's minds when they first saw it. Actually, blows my mind, still, to be honest. We've got space—tons of space—outside and in. Upstairs, the boys and I took over a whole room and created our own man cave—pool table, huge flat-screen TV, video games, minifridge, the works. Outside we have a front lawn, and right across the narrow paved roadway leading into our development there's a large patch of green where Johnny and Jason can throw the football and shag flies.

In the back of our house, we have a wide patio, deck, and full-size swimming pool. Late in the day, especially sum-mer afternoons when the temperature drops to a balmy 103, Julie and I sit outside in a couple of lounge chairs while the boys splash around in the pool. They play water basket-ball or challenge each other to swimming races. Every so often, when the heat gets oppressive, I'll roll into the pool myself, and if they ask—they usually don't—I'll suggest a few swimming pointers. All of this—my world, my retreat, the desert rock shimmering behind us in the background the color of rust—sits exactly three minutes from the studio where I broadcast my nightly syndicated sports talk show. It is, as Andrew would've said, "grand."

Andrew didn't love Vegas, but I know he would have liked

this house. He would've felt comfortable here. He would've gawked at the expanse of it, the man cave we created, the open area downstairs, the kitchen flowing into the family room. A perfect place to entertain, he would've thought, both homey and a great party house.

Even more, though, he would've loved sitting with me outside and watching the kids romp in the pool.

Sometimes when Julie and I relax outside on those summer afternoons, I remember how Andrew and I would sit in the backyard of our house in Sherman Oaks, near Fox Sports Radio, watching Johnny and Jason play football or baseball or NASCAR. He would watch them, and he would laugh and applaud, and an expression of sheer joy would erupt across his face. He could hardly contain himself. Watching my kids then, he became a kid himself. I can hear his voice: *I love seeing you with your kids, JT. This is really what it's all about.*

I can't say I remember everything Andrew taught me, but I will never forget this:

It's about family. It's all that matters.

And your family includes your friends.

This afternoon, late in August, the Vegas heat beats down hard. The light surrounds Julie and me, vibrating orange. I look over at Julie in her lounge chair, dozing. Next to her, between us, another lounge chair sits empty.

I squint and—I know the desert and the sweltering heat can play tricks on you; I've heard of images appearing, mirages— suddenly Andrew appears next to me, filling up that vacant lounge chair, all three hundred pounds of him. His full blond hair, long, out of control, falls down to his shoulders, and he laughs, his eyes squinting, his fleshy face jiggling in ecstasy, roaring now and pointing at the kids, who splash wildly in the pool, jumping up and shooting baskets at the plastic basketball hoop that bobs a few feet away.

"Yeah, babe."

"Hey, bro."

"You did it, babe. You fucking did it. Good job. You got to exactly where you need to be."

I nod. Sweat pools up on my forehead and drips into my eyes.

Andrew tilts his head toward my sons and then turns to me, shades his eyes with his beefy hand, and, his face covered in shadow, says, "Everything you learned in your life...everything that's part of you...you're gonna hand off to them."

I feel wetness douse my cheeks, sweat mixed with my tears.

"Don't drop the ball, bro. Keep it going."

I'm afraid to move, to blink. I'm afraid that if I do, Andrew will go away. But I know, in some ways, he never will, and so I have that. And I swear to myself that I will do the best I can to hand off what I have learned to my sons and to the people I mentor and to anyone else who will listen or read.

But late at night, when I'm alone, blasting through my show, my voice bellowing in the dark, I can't help thinking that he's still out there listening and that Bobby's voice will echo through my headset, "JT, there's a guy on line one. Says something about a playbook."

Andrew, a dash of Tabasco, a shot of Patrón Silver, a chilled wedge of grapefruit.

I raise my glass.

This one's for you.

Acknowledgments

JT

To Alan Eisenstock: I will be forever grateful for the way you made this such an incredible experience and I will always treasure our powerful friendship.

To my broadcasting agents, Lisa and Matt Miller of Miller Broadcast Management. We've been through so much together; you've helped me grow both personally and professionally. Everything in my career has happened because of your guidance.

To my literary agent, Wendy Sherman. I appreciate how your instinct and expertise made this story come to life.

To my editor, Kate Hartson. Your enthusiasm and heartfelt passion throughout this process has been incredible.

To everyone at Hachette and Center Street, in particular Harry Helm, Andrea Glickson, Shannon Stowe, Sarah Beatty, and Lauren Rohrig.

Delta Kappa Tau Fraternity Chapter at SUNY Geneseo: To all my fraternity brothers and our strong past and whose "bonds of steel shall never weaken."

New York

Jim Baxter, Geoff Hayden, Tom Wisniewski, Chris Ferro, Aret Shahinian, Louis Migliaccio, Greg Eddy, Jim Brown, Jim Anderson, Robert Newlands, Mike DeSando, Mike Binning, Michael "Rocket" Rose, Tom Byrne, Steve Cohen, George O'Brien, Michael Coppola, Ken Rodriguez, Michael Gerber, Bob Bergsten, Mike Eble, Bob

Fischer, Jim Kaelin, Jay Malone, Andy Maffett, Dan Herc, Joe Hickey, Bilbo, Chris McCrary, John Maloney, John Sennett, James Schneider, the Dooling brothers, Rick Burke, Tracey Bowden, and Billy Zagger.

California

San Diego

Bob Griffin, JD Crow, John Butler, Mike Hochbrueckner and the Sea Monsters, Jim "Big Daddy" McCullough, Mark McCord, Steve Ahn, Roger Grove, Charles Singer, Charlie Simmer, Tim Cusick, Chip Ruysschaert, Tom Schrader, Paul Van Vessen, Roger Guy English, John Craft, Mike Cannon, Keith Dunlea, Brad Flipse, Kurt Finley, and Bob and Jannine Meyerott for always treating me like a member of your family.

Bay Area

Tony Cambareri, Tony Salvadore, Lee Hammer, Michelle Martin, Steve Mortara, Chris Eaton, Jeff Williams, Chris Callahan, Ken White, and Ricky and Tina Ricardo.

Los Angeles

Brian Burkhardt, Don Tardino, and Gary Kawesch.

Tomm Looney, the iconic voice of my radio world.

Dave Coelho, I will always consider you my younger brother.

Sam Betesh, what a ride it's been, and the best is yet to come.

Las Vegas

Todd Parmelee, Bobby Machado, Brady Kannon, John Saccenti, Chris Bruno, Christian Toner, Rudy Postigo, Lou Paone, Mike Pritchard, Dave Markall, Scott Ghertner, John O'Donnell, Dave Herlong, Mike Diamond, Rich Kenny, Jim Gallo, Paul Howard, Steve Cofield, Dave Cokin, Bernie Fratto, the Maloofs, Kerrie Burke, Danny DeFreitas, Jon Hait, Tony Bonnici, and the entire Lotus Broadcasting family.

Radio

Julie Talbot, Kraig Kitchin, Tom Lee, Annie Zidarevich, Kurt Kretzchmar, Charlie Barker, Chris Myers, Mike Pearson, Elan Kriegel, Ryan Payne, Vito Violante, Robert Grusman, Jake Warner, Robert Guerra, Roj Grobes, Scott Ferrall, Steve Czaban, Jorge Sedano, Bruce Jacobs, Greg Toohey, Erik Peterson, Vladimir Louissaint, Eddie Garcia, Michael Lingard, Michael Coover, Dan Beyer, Krystal Fernandez, Steve Stillwell, Mike Dunsmore, Brian Cox, Craig Sheeman, James Washington, Sean Farnham, Deb Carson, Karen Kay, Scott Kaplan, Nate Lundy, Peter Burns, Charlie Parker, Walter Pasacrita, Bill Schoening, Damon Bruce, Rick Scott, Dave Sniff, and Joe Petrovich.

Al Davis, Jon Gruden, Jim Brown, Fred Bilitnikoff, Pete Rose, Digger Phelps, Charles Barkley, and Don King.

Oakland Raiders

Mark Davis, Amy Trask, George Atkinson, Marc Badain, John and Jim Otten, Vittorio DeBartolo, Brad Phinney, Greg Papa, Cliff Branch, Morris Bradshaw, Lincoln Kennedy, Napoleon McCallum, Shane Lechler, Jerry Knaak, and to the Black Hole, Football's Most Notorious Fans.

Callers

I will always appreciate and respect the fanatics who take the time to call in and sound off like they have a pair.

To Ben E. Jet, your friendship and never-ending support means more to me than you will ever know.

To the Mayor of Poway, Raider Mort, Ted "Trigger" Hentschell, Sugar White Mike, John in Frasier, Butch from the Cape, Mick in Hayward, and the thousands of listeners who picked up the phone and voiced their opinions on my radio shows, THANK YOU.

Team Ashwood

Sandra, your courage and friendship continues to amaze me. Andrew was never happier than when he was with you.

Bruce Allen, your leadership qualities are a guiding force in my life.

Mike Drescher and Jeff Rowe. You are two of the best men I've ever met. Because of Andrew we will always be connected. Thank you for all of your help.

Chris and Spencer Stiles. Andrew was so proud of his nephews, and I know his passion for the Green Bay Packers will continue through both of you.

Timm Amundson; Gabe Hobbs; Bob Passwaters; The Human Calculator; Scott Flansburg; Jay Glazer; Sunil Sujan; Jim Wimpress; William "Radio Bill" Hamrick; Kipper McGee; Tim Ryan; Ann Ashwood, Amy Ashwood, and Lorry Stiles, Andrew's sisters.

William Scull, RIP and thanks for the Rolling Stones tickets!

Family

To my sisters Dana Conway and husband Paul, Jill Burke and husband Ed.

Aunt Inez and Uncle Bill, Uncle Gene and Aunt Valerie, Uncle Tom and Aunt Wilma.

Cousins Shawn, Laura, Dan, Gene, Andrea, Susie, and their families, and my in-laws Mike and Judy Lumpp, and sister-in-law Jodie and her husband Greg Caldwell.

To all my nieces, nephews, and goddaughters, CJ, Brianna, Corey, Grace, Casey, Chloe, Claire, Gabriella, Nick, Frankie, Joey, and Audrey.

To my parents, John and Maureen.

Finally, to my wife, Julie, and our sons, John and Jason. You fulfill me every day. I could not have done this without you.

ALAN

I owe a tremendous debt of gratitude to all who participated in this project and supported me during the research and writing of *The Handoff.*

To John "JT the Brick" Tournour, thank you for your unflinching courage, enormous patience, and unshakable trust. I love you, brother.

To the two women who made this happen—Wendy Sherman for seeing and Kate Hartson for believing.

To everyone at Hachette and Center Street, including but not limited to Harry Helm, Andrea Glickson, Shannon Stowe, Sarah Beatty, and Lauren Rohrig.

To Julie Talbot for your blessing.

To Lisa Miller and Matt Miller for being so thorough, caring, accessible, and enthusiastic.

To Sandra Ashwood for your support, guidance, and trust.

To Tomm Looney, Jim Baxter, Sunil Sujan, and especially Jeff Rowe and Michael Drescher.

To Maureen and John Tournour.

To Julie Tournour for, well, everything.

To David Ritz for dragging me out of the darkness of the writer's rabbit hole and into the light about a million times.

To the "A Team"—Madeline and Phil Schwarzman, Susan Pomerantz and George Weinberger, Susan Baskin and Richard Gerwitz, the Barrabees, Steve Marks, Marty Nadler, Gary Meisel, Linda Nussbaum, Randy Turtle, and Jim and Jay Eisenstock.

To Katie O'Laughlin, thank you for allowing me to accompany you to chemotherapy and for becoming cancer free.

To Frieda Agler, I cheer you on every day.

To the greatest family on earth, my Fab Four, Bobbie, Jonah, Kiva, and Snickers Eisenstock, and in memory of Z. and GG.

Finally, to Andrew Ashwood. Your immense spirit will live forever.

A portion of the proceeds from The Handoff *will go to City of Hope in memory of Andrew Ashwood.*